Oliver Wendell Holmes

Sage of the Supreme Court

OXFORD
PORTRAITS

Oliver Wendell Holmes

Sage of the Supreme Court

G. Edward White

Oxford University Press
New York • Oxford

In memory of Frances McCafferty White

OXFORD
UNIVERSITY PRESS

Oxford   New York
Athens   Auckland   Bangkok   Bogotá   Buenos Aires   Calcutta
Cape Town   Chennai   Dar es Salaam   Delhi   Florence   Hong Kong   Istanbul
Karachi   Kuala Lumpur   Madrid   Melbourne   Mexico City   Mumbai
Nairobi   Paris   São Paulo   Singapore   Taipei   Tokyo   Toronto   Warsaw
and associated companies in
Berlin   Ibadan

Copyright © 2000 by G. Edward White
Published by Oxford University Press, Inc.
198 Madison Avenue, New York, New York 10016
Web site: www.oup.com

Oxford is a registered trademark of Oxford University Press

Design and layout: Greg Wozney
Picture research: Lisa Kirchner

Library of Congress Cataloging-in-Publication Data
White, G. Edward.
Oliver Wendell Holmes: sage of the Supreme Court / G. Edward White.
p. cm.
Includes bibliographical references and index.
Summary : A biography of the well-known philosopher and judge, with emphasis
on his influential thirty-year tenure as an associate justice of the United States
Supreme Court.
ISBN 0-19-511667-4 (lib. : alk. paper)
1. Holmes, Oliver Wendell, 1841–1935 Juvenile literature.
2. Judges—United States Biography Juvenile Literature.
[1. Holmes, Oliver Wendell, 1841–1935. 2. Judges.] I. Title.
KF8745.H6W473   1999
347.73'2634—dc21   99-34529
[B]   CIP

9 8 7 6 5 4 3 2 1

Printed in the United States of America
on acid-free paper

On the cover: Oliver Wendell Holmes in 1931, the twenty-ninth year of his tenure
  on the Supreme Court.
Frontispiece: Holmes at the age of 90.

CONTENTS

Justice Holmes leaves the Capitol, where the Supreme Court met during the time he served on it, on the arm of his close friend Justice Louis D. Brandeis. The occasion was Holmes's 90th birthday. He is the only Supreme Court justice to have served on the Court at that age.

PROLOGUE: THE 90TH-BIRTHDAY ADDRESS

The old man sat in his favorite chair in his study. He had a shock of white hair, a long white mustache that flared up at the ends, and piercing eyes that gave him a fierce expression. The year was 1931, and most men favored collars with the ends folded down, but he wore an old-fashioned type with the ends turned up and the tie visible, wrapped around his neck. He also wore an old-fashioned long coat with a vest. He had gotten dressed up to speak on the radio.

Oliver Wendell Holmes Jr. was a justice of the Supreme Court of the United States. The occasion of his radio speech was his 90th birthday, which was being celebrated because he was the oldest active judge in the history of the Supreme Court. At the time, Holmes was also the most famous living judge in America, and very possibly the most famous judge in U.S. history.

Radio was still new in 1931. The first U.S. radio station had begun broadcasting only in 1920. Although the number of stations had grown significantly during the 1920s, radios were still large and clumsy, difficult to carry around. There were no radios in cars and no portable transistor radios. When Americans listened to a broadcast in those days, they gathered in a living room or a public place and sat around the set. Sometimes it was necessary for everyone who wanted to listen to have a separate pair of very large and bulky earphones. When Holmes spoke on the radio, about 500 people gathered in one of the main buildings of Harvard Law School, where he had been a student in the 1860s, to hear the broadcast. Holmes's address was broadcast by the Columbia Broadcasting System (CBS), one of the three nationwide radio networks in existence at the time. It was not unusual for a network to do a report about law or the Supreme Court of the United States. It was unusual, however, for a nationwide radio network to celebrate the birthday of a Supreme Court justice; most people would not have been able even to name the other justices who sat with Holmes on the Court.

Charles Evans Hughes, the chief justice of the United States, introduced Holmes to the radio audience: "It is difficult for one who is in daily and intimate association with him to think of great age, as he is a constant contradiction of all that great age usually implies…. In his important work, he is indefatigable. Every case that is presented to the Court arouses in him such immediate and earnest response that it is almost impossible to realize that in his service in the Supreme Court of the United States and the Supreme Judicial Court of Massachusetts he has been listening to argument for almost fifty years."

In his address Holmes did not talk about the details of his long life. He did not dwell on his many accomplishments. Instead, on that Sunday night of March 8, 1931, he talked about aging, about contemplating death, and about continuing to work.

> In this symposium my part is only to sit in silence. To express one's feelings as the end draws near is too intimate a task. But I may mention one thought that occurs to me as a listener-in. The riders

Justice Oliver Wendell Holmes, pictured on his 90th birthday in the study of his home in Washington, D.C., where he wrote his opinions as an associate justice of the U.S. Supreme Court. Holmes was in the 30th year of his tenure on the Court.

in the race do not stop short when they reach the goal. There is a little finishing canter before coming to a standstill. There is time to hear the kind voice of friends and to say to oneself: The work is done. But just as one says that, the answer comes: The race is over, but the work never is done while the power to work remains. The canter that brings you to a stand-still need not be only coming to rest. It cannot be while you still live. For to live is to function. That is all there is in living. And so I end with a line from a Latin poet who uttered the message more than fif-teen hundred years ago: "Death plucks my ear and says, 'Live—I am coming.'"

That was Holmes's entire address. One might have thought that instead of a Supreme Court justice, Holmes was a poet or a writer, interested in philosophical and liter-ary matters. And, in fact, Holmes was as much interested in philosophy and literature as he was in law. But he had become a public figure as a judge, and he had quite self-consciously given up those other pursuits in order to con-centrate on law. Yet his long service in the legal profes-sion—as a young lawyer in Boston, legal scholar, professor at Harvard Law School, judge on the Supreme Judicial Court of Massachusetts, and for 30 years justice of the Supreme Court—never quenched his desire to write and to philoso-phize. He had grafted those pursuits onto his legal career, and his skills at writing and at glimpsing the philosophical foundations of law were to single him out among his fellow judges.

There was another temptation Holmes felt and one that he had alluded to in quoting the line from the anonymous Latin poet. The original meaning of the line, in a poem entitled "The Syrian Dancing Girl," had been to praise the idea of living life to the fullest, because death is bound to come. In his radio address Holmes had changed the mean-ing by associating life with "work." So Death, in Holmes's version of the poem, could have been saying, "Get back to

work." But in the original version Death was saying something more like "Eat, drink, and be merry." Holmes knew
the temptation to "live" in the original sense of the poem
very well. He loved adventure and romance, and although
he spent most of his life with books and papers, writing
opinions and letters, working in comparative solitude, his
zest for what he once called "high and dangerous action"
remained with him. The story of Holmes's life is also a
story about how a man who spent 50 years as a judge,
largely isolated from the worlds of action and adventure,
could nonetheless be thought of by many citizens as a
romantic figure, a kind of American hero.

Holmes and his mother, Amelia Jackson Holmes, in 1858, when informal photographs were rare.

THE FAMILY LEGACY

On the night of his 90th-birthday address, Holmes invited a friend, Harold Laski, to listen to the broadcast at his home. The two had first met when Holmes was in his early 70s and Laski in his late 20s. Laski was a native of England and spent most of his career as a professor of law and government in British universities, but he corresponded very frequently with Holmes, and the two men valued each other's friendship. In 1948, 13 years after Holmes's death, Laski told a story about the night he had listened to Holmes's birthday address. "When the engineer had taken the radio apparatus away," Laski said, Holmes returned to his favorite armchair by the fire. "As I looked at him, his eyes seemed far away, and the swift realization that I was watching the face of a very old man, very greatly moved, kept me silent." Then, Laski continued:

> I saw a new light come into those blue-gray eyes, and then a gay smile that played over all his features. The words he spoke as that smile met the flash of those vivid eyes are as living today in my ears as they were almost seventeen years ago. "When I came back from the Civil War," Holmes

said, "my father asked me what I was going to do, and I told him I was going to the Harvard Law School. 'Pooh!' said my father, 'What's the use of going to the Harvard Law School? A lawyer cannot be a great man.'" Then there came into his voice an almost wistful tenderness. "I wish," he continued, "that my father could have listened tonight for only two or three minutes. Then I could have thumbed my nose at him."

Harold Laski liked to exaggerate, and his recollection of what Holmes said might not have been completely accurate. When Holmes's father, Oliver Wendell Holmes Sr., died in 1894, his son was already a justice of the Supreme Judicial Court of Massachusetts, the author of the celebrated book *The Common Law,* and a former member of the Harvard Law School faculty. Some people in legal circles might have already thought him a "great man." But if Laski's report is correct, it captures something of how Holmes felt about his career. For all his accomplishments in the legal profession, Holmes did not become a "great man" until very late in his life, after he had served on the Supreme Court of the United States for more than 10 years and was older than 70. In fact, when his father died, Holmes experienced the frustration of realizing that his father was much more famous than he was. Even when Holmes was appointed to the Supreme Court in 1901, he was known to the general public primarily as the son of Oliver Wendell Holmes Sr. The central theme of Holmes's family history was his struggle to distance himself from his famous father and at the same time to become equally famous himself.

When Oliver Wendell Holmes Jr. was born on March 8, 1841, in Boston, his father, then 36 years old, was beginning to make a name for himself in three different areas. He had received a medical degree from Harvard in 1834 and was a practicing doctor in Boston. In addition, in 1838 he had begun a career as a public lecturer on the Lyceum Circuit, traveling as a guest speaker to small towns to talk on various subjects as a means of educating the residents in an age in which there were few other forms of public entertainment.

People flocked to listen to him, not because he was a doctor but because he was a poet. In 1830, at the age of 21, Holmes Sr. had published a poem, "Old Ironsides," protesting the proposed destruction of a Revolutionary War ship, the *Constitution,* which lay in Boston Harbor. The poem was so well received that it helped save the ship. During his years as a medical student and doctor, Holmes Sr. continued to write poetry and literary essays. In 1849, when his son Wendell was 8, Holmes Sr. was appointed professor of anatomy at Harvard Medical School, which freed him from having to practice medicine and allowed him more time for his lectures and writing.

In 1857 Holmes Sr. wrote a series of essays entitled "The Autocrat of the Breakfast Table" that appeared in the *Atlantic Monthly,* a literary magazine that he had helped found. The essays, set in a fictional rooming house, were a series of monologues and conversations by a narrator, the Autocrat, who holds forth on a variety of topics, such as religion, the art of conversation, "vulgarisms" in speech, and "pseudo-science" in medicine. Their combination of learning, wit, and observations about the world of 19th-century Boston made them tremendously popular. They were collected in book form, and a second series followed, collected in 1872 as *The Poet at the Breakfast Table.* By the time of his death, Holmes Sr.'s essays, his editorship of the *Atlantic Monthly,* and his poetry had made him one of the best-known American writers of the 19th century.

There were other members of the household in which Oliver Wendell Holmes Jr. grew up, but none was as important to him as his father. His mother, Amelia Jackson Holmes, was by all accounts a self-effacing, affectionate,

A caricature of Holmes Sr. on the cover of Vanity Fair *magazine's June 7, 1862, issue. Five years earlier he had founded the* Atlantic Monthly *and begun his series of essays featuring "The Autocrat of the Breakfast Table," which earned him a national reputation as a wit and man of letters.*

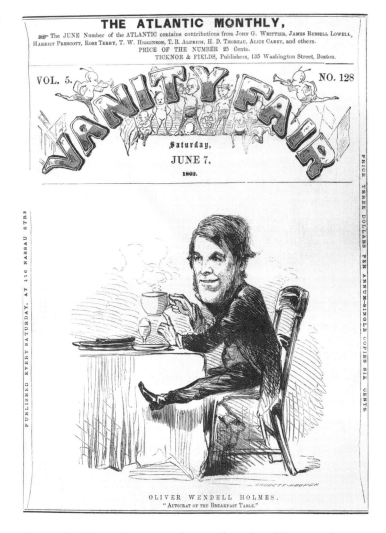

THE ATLANTIC MONTHLY,

The JUNE Number of the ATLANTIC contains contributions from JOHN G. WHITTIER, JAMES RUSSELL LOWELL, HARRIET PRESCOTT, ROSE TERRY, T. W. HIGGINSON, T. B. ALDRICH, H. D. THOREAU, ALICE CAREY, and others.

PRICE OF THE NUMBER 25 Cents.

TICKNOR & FIELDS, Publishers, 135 Washington Street, Boston.

VOL. 5.   NO. 128

Saturday, JUNE 7, 1862.

PUBLISHED EVERY SATURDAY, AT 116 NASSAU STRE

PRICE THREE DOLLARS PER ANNUM—SINGLE COPIES SIX CENTS

OLIVER WENDELL HOLMES.
"AUTOCRAT OF THE BREAKFAST TABLE."

devoted wife and parent who preferred public attention to be directed at someone other than herself. Holmes Jr.'s letters to his mother make it clear that he was prepared to unburden himself of his doubts or fears to her—he wrote her of such feelings while serving in the Civil War—but she remained a background figure, whereas his father was someone whose life and career would serve as a foil for his own. As for his younger sister, Amelia, who was born in 1843, and his younger brother, Edward, born in 1846, they did not seem to be pivotal figures in his life. He did not mention them in the autobiographical sketch he wrote on graduating for Harvard College in 1861, and he rarely mentioned them in the numerous letters he wrote later in his life. Both were to die at comparatively young ages, Edward at the age of 38 in 1884 and Amelia at 46 in 1889. The principal story that has been passed on about Wendell, as Holmes Jr. came to be called, and his family circle notes Wendell's tendency, at the breakfast table, to end his sentences with a "but" so that he could continue to hold the center of attention while he thought up something new to say. The point of the story was not that his mother, sister, or brother would take over the conversation. It was his father whom Wendell was trying to forestall: Holmes Sr.'s reputation was that of one of the most talkative and entertaining personalities in Boston.

The first major event that distanced Holmes from his father came during his time as an undergraduate at Harvard College. Holmes went to Harvard, as he later said, as a matter of course. His father and both of his grandfathers had gone there. He did not find his undergraduate education—which was mainly a continuation of the drills in Latin, Greek, ancient history, and mathematics he had experienced at private school—particularly stimulating. Neither did he enjoy the method by which students were ranked, which consisted of a series of credits for successful class recitations and demerits for various types of misconduct, which included being rude in class, messing up dormitory rooms, making noise at night, and failing to attend meals or functions.

After three years of uneven attention to his studies and occasional disciplinary problems (he once was censured for breaking windows in another student's dormitory room and once for "repeated and gross indecorum" in a moral philosophy class), Holmes finally, in the spring of his senior year, found a subject that inspired him. Unfortunately, from the perspective of his father, the subject had nothing to do with his education. It was the issue of slavery and the coming of the Civil War that captured Holmes's attention.

Holmes Sr. was not particularly supportive of the abolitionist movement to outlaw slavery, which had sprung up in the Boston area in the late 1850s and early 1860s. Holmes Sr. felt no particular outrage at those Southern states that practiced slavery, but Amelia Jackson Holmes did, and abolitionism became an important cause for Wendell Holmes. Through a close friend at Harvard, Penrose Hallowell, Holmes became involved with a group of young men who supported abolitionist activity. As relations between the North and South worsened in the spring of 1861—the year he was scheduled to graduate from Harvard—Wendell became increasingly drawn to what eventually became a volunteer war effort by Massachusetts regiments pledged to join the newly constituted Union army, which came into being after the secession of the Confederate states that spring. In April Wendell, Hallowell, and several other classmates left Harvard and enlisted in the Fourth Battalion of Massachusetts Volunteers. They were assigned to guard duty at Boston Harbor. Holmes made no effort to contact Harvard before leaving; he believed he was involved in more important activities now.

Holmes Sr. was not pleased about his son's enlistment. Nonetheless, he recognized that his views were likely to have little influence on his son, and he focused his efforts on attempting to reestablish contact between Wendell and Harvard College. Eventually, he helped persuade the Harvard authorities to allow Wendell and several of his volunteer classmates—who had found, to their dismay, that the Fourth Battalion was not going to see any military action outside of Boston—to return to Harvard and take their examinations. Holmes graduated from Harvard in June 1861 with the rest of his class. He did not rank as high in his class as he would have before leaving, however. Class ranks at the time were determined by a combination of grades and "deportment," and Holmes received academic demerits for his absence from college during the spring.

Holmes's service in the Civil War, which began the summer after his college graduation and lasted until 1864, significantly contributed to the process by which he eventually declared his independence from his father. At the outset of Holmes's wartime service, however, it appeared that this grand gesture would not result in any exposure to combat, because the Fourth Battalion had orders to remain in the Boston area, far from the center of wartime action, the Middle Atlantic states.

On learning this news, Holmes, Hallowell, and several other members of their Harvard class resigned from the Fourth Battalion in June 1861 and sought to secure commissions in the 20th Regiment of Massachusetts Volunteers, which was expected to go south and fight. It took some time, however, for Holmes's commission to come through; he was one of the last of his classmates accepted into the 20th Regiment. (His father, despite his reservations about the war, had quietly intervened with the governor of Massachusetts to try to get Wendell a commission.) Eventually, in late July, it came through, and by September Holmes was preparing to march south with the 20th Regiment to see action in the area of Washington, D.C.

Earlier, in July, Wendell Holmes had written an autobiographical sketch for his Harvard class album. Most of the sketch traced his family history and included references to his father; his grandfather Abiel Holmes, a Congregational minister and the author of a well-known early 19th-century guidebook, *The Annals of America;* his grandfather Judge Charles Jackson; and one of his great-grandmothers, the poet Anne Bradstreet. "Our family has been in the habit of receiving a college education," he noted, "and I came of course in my turn." He mentioned that he had been elected Class Poet and added, "The tendencies of the family and of myself have a strong natural bent for literature." But then

Holmes turned to the future rather than the past. "At present," Holmes wrote, "I am trying for a commission in one of the Massachusetts Regiments.... If I survive the war I expect to study law as my profession or at least for a starting point."

Oliver Wendell Holmes Sr. was probably not pleased to read that his son hoped to engage in active service in the Civil War, although he expected Wendell soon to go south with a Massachusetts regiment. He was also probably unenthusiastic on reading Wendell's announcement that he hoped to study law. The elder Holmes had tried law school himself, entering Harvard Law School in the fall of 1829. By January 1830 he was writing a friend, "I am sick at heart of this place and almost everything connected with it. I know not what the temple of the law may be to those who have entered it, but to me it seems very cold and cheerless at the threshold." Six months later he had quit law school to become a medical student.

In the fall of 1861, however, Wendell Holmes probably cared very little about his father's attitude toward the

Holmes sits third from the left in this 1869 reunion photograph of the officers of the 20th Regiment of Massachusetts Volunteers. At the age of 28 he had already faced the threat of death during the Civil War.

prospect of his studying law. He was preoccupied with the details of his forthcoming action in combat. From Boston the 20th Regiment, part of the Army of the Potomac, had moved to Camp Kalorama, on the heights of a section of Washington called Georgetown, where they met other regiments under the command of General George McClellan. The Army of the Potomac's mission was to protect the city of Washington from Confederate raids and to make successful excursions into Virginia, eventually reaching the Confederate capital of Richmond. For a variety of reasons, that mission was never accomplished, and in the course of the next three and a half years Wendell Holmes had a first-hand picture of the horrors of war. Despite the severe trials, he came to feel that his experience in the Civil War was one of the most meaningful and uplifting ones of his life. War, he later wrote, was "horrible and dull," but its "message was divine."

An Autobiographical Sketch

Although Holmes spent most of the last month of his spring semester with the Fourth Battalion of Massachusetts Volunteers guarding Boston Harbor, he still graduated from Harvard on June 22, 1861. Ten days later he wrote this account of his life for the class album.

I, Oliver Wendell Holmes, Jr., was born March 8, 1841, in Boston. My father was born in Cambridge, graduated at Harvard, studied medicine in Paris and returning to Boston practiced as a physician there a number of years. Giving this up, however, he has since supported himself by acting as a professor of the Medical School of Harvard College, by lecturing, and by writing a number of books. In 1840 he married Amelia Lee Jackson, daughter of Judge Jackson of Boston, where he has since resided. All my three names designate families from which I am descended.... Of my grandfather Abiel Holmes, an account may be found in the biographical dictionaries ... as also of my other grandfather Charles Jackson.... Some of my ancestors have fought in the Revolution; among the great grandmothers of the family were Dorothy Quincy and Anne Bradstreet ("the tenth Muse") ... but these things can be picked up from other sources .... My grandfather A. Holmes was graduated from Yale in 1783.... Various Wendells and Olivers will be found in the triennial [of Harvard University graduates], as also various Jacksons.... Our family has been in the habit of receiving a college education, and I came of course in my turn, as my grandfathers, fathers, and uncles had been before me. I've always lived in Boston and went first to a woman's school (preschool through early elementary) there, then Rev. T. R. Sullivan's, then to E. S. Dixwell's (Private Latin School) and thence to College. I never had any business but that of a student before coming to College; which I did with the majority of our class in July [1857]. I was while in College, a member and editor of the Institute (had somewhat to do with our two private clubs), of the Hasty Pudding, the Porcellian, the [Phi Beta Kappa Society], and the "Christian Union," not that I considered my life justified belonging to the latter, but because I wished to bear testimony in favor of a Religious society founded on liberal principles in distinction to the more "orthodox" and sectarian platform of the "Christian Brethren." I was editor in the Senior year of the Harvard Magazine.... I was author of an article on Plato which took the prize as the best article by an undergraduate ... in the "University Quarterly."... When the war broke out I joined the "4th Battalion of Infantry" and went down to Fort Independence expecting when drilled to go south (as a private). While at the fort and after we were ordered up I had to patch up a Class Poem as quickly and well as I could under the circumstances, since I had been elected to the office before going.... We stayed about a month at the Fort and then I came to Boston and on Classday (a week and a half ago) I delivered my poem.... The tendencies of the family and of myself have a strong natural bent for literature ... at present I am trying for a commission in one of the Massachusetts Regiments, however, and I hope to go south before very long. If I survive the war I expect to study law as my profession or at least for a starting point.

(in haste)
O. W. Holmes, Jr.
July 2, 1861

(N.B. I may say I don't believe in gushing much in these College Biog's and think a dry statement much fitter. Also I am too busy to say more if I would.)

Holmes in the first year of his Civil War service, which began in July 1861. Three months later he would narrowly escape death in the battle of Ball's Bluff, where he was shot in the chest, the bullet just missing his heart and lungs.

Our Hearts Were Touched with Fire: The Civil War Years

In April 1864, Wendell Holmes described his experience in the Civil War as "a crusade in the cause of the whole civilized world." He had gone to war for two related reasons. He enlisted because he opposed slavery but also because dedication to such noble causes was an obligation of young, educated Boston gentlemen. Both of these reasons were part of his romantic view of participation in the war. He was going off on a great adventure, a crusade.

As a boy and young man in Boston, Wendell had had little contact with African Americans, and very probably none with slaves. He had known some Southerners at Harvard, and although there is evidence in his undergraduate essays that he was repelled by the practice of slavery, he did not shun or condemn his Southern classmates because their families had slaves. His decision to actively join the war effort came after his close friend Penrose Hallowell had urged him on by example.

Twenty years after he had mustered out of military service, Holmes characterized his generation, who had "carried on the war," as having "been set apart by its experience." "Through our great good fortune," he said, "in our youth our hearts were touched with fire…. We have seen with our own eyes … the snowy heights of honor."

In those passages Holmes made the Civil War sound as if it had been the great adventure he expected it to be. But the reality of his wartime experience was different. That war was one of the last in which men still fought with bayonets; there were no airplanes, tanks, or other motorized vehicles. Campaigns took place largely on foot, with horseback combat being reserved for a select group of officers. But at the same time, rifle and cannon fire were common, and deadly bullets and shells, the kind that blew their victims apart, had been introduced. Huge numbers of men fought on both sides; some battles resulted in casualties numbering in the tens of thousands. Because long-range surface weapons were still uncommon, and air attacks nonexistent, battles had to be fought at close range. The result was that few men could avoid being exposed to the deadly fire of their enemies. In many respects the Civil War was the most gruesome war in U.S. history. And it went on, with almost no letup in fighting, for more than four years.

The chances of not being wounded, for anyone who fought in an infantry regiment for four years, were small. Holmes was wounded three times. In his very first battle he was nearly killed, taking a bullet in his chest that somehow missed his heart and lungs. The 20th Regiment, after arriving in Washington, had been instructed to cross the Potomac River from Maryland into Virginia in October 1861 to discourage Confederate forces from coming any closer to the capital. The regiment found no Confederates on the Virginia side of the river and camped for the night on a plateau known as Ball's Bluff. Meanwhile the Confederates had learned that there were no reinforcements behind Holmes's regiment and that the river would prevent an easy escape. They ambushed the regiment and drove them back across the river, killing or wounding more than half of the 1,700 Union soldiers camped at Ball's Bluff. Holmes was shot through the chest. A fellow soldier carried him to the rear and extracted the bullet. The wound was severe enough that he was sent home at the end of October and did not resume active service until March 1862.

After he returned to action, Holmes entered into a stage of his wartime career that was even more unpleasant and frightening. Between March and the end of August 1862, the 20th Regiment was involved in the Peninsula Campaign. This was a persistent but ultimately unsuccessful effort by the Army of the Potomac to march from the Tidewater area of Virginia, through low, swampy terrain, toward Richmond, the capital of the Confederacy, in the hope of capturing that city. Progress through the peninsula east of Richmond was painfully slow: Holmes's regiment encountered mosquitoes, mud, dysentery, and periodic bloody fighting. After one battle Holmes wrote his parents, "As you go through the woods you stumble constantly, and if after dark … perhaps tread on the swollen bodies already fly blown and decaying, of men shot in the head, back, or bowels." At the end of August, the Peninsula Campaign was suddenly abandoned, and the 20th Regiment moved north to defend the city of Washington from possible attacks by Confederate generals Stonewall Jackson and Robert E. Lee.

The return of the Army of the Potomac to the Washington area and the approach of Confederate forces led to one of the major battles of the Civil War, the Battle of Antietam Creek, near Sharpsburg, Maryland, about a mile from the Potomac River. In that battle, which took place on September 17, 1862, more than 6,000 men from both sides were killed and more than 17,000 wounded. Holmes was one of those wounded, this time shot through the back of the neck. Once again the bullet had missed any vital organs. Holmes was taken to a farmhouse that served as a temporary hospital, had his wound plugged with lint, was

"I Thought I Was Dying"

During the Civil War soldiers took laudanum, a variant of opium used as a painkiller, to relieve suffering if they were fatally wounded—an overdose was lethal. At Ball's Bluff in October 1861, Holmes had taken a small bottle of laudanum with him into combat. The doctor who treated him for his chest wound after the battle discouraged him from using it, and eventually took the bottle from him.

This account was found on separate sheets of paper tucked into the back of Holmes's Civil War diary; it was probably written after his military service had concluded. Unlike most of the other entries, it is written in a more polished style and includes not only descriptions of wartime events but also reflections on them. The letters and diary found in Holmes's papers after his death were not complete versions of his Civil War correspondence, and he told friends late in his life that he was doing his best to forestall biographers by destroying papers he did not want made public.

I felt as if a horse had kicked me.... I felt for the laudanum (tincture of opium, a poison) and ... determined to wait till pain or sinking strength warned me of the end being near.... I called [a doctor] and gave him my address and told him ... if I died to write home & tell 'em I done my duty—I was very anxious they should know that— and then I imparted to him my laudanum scheme—This he dissuaded and gave me a dose of some opiate ... and when I slumbered I believe he prigged the bottle.

Of course when I thought I was dying the reflection that the majority vote of the civilized world declared that with my opinions I was en route for Hell came up with painful distinctness—Perhaps the first impulse was tremulous, but then I said—by Jove, I die like a soldier anyhow—I was shot in the breast doing my duty up to the hub. Afraid?

No, I am proud—then I thought I couldn't be guilty of a deathbed recantation; father and I had talked of that and were agreed that it generally meant nothing more than a cowardly giving way to fear. Besides, thought I, can I recant if I want to, has the approach of death changed my beliefs much? & to this I answered, No. Then came in my philosophy—I am to take a leap in the dark—but now as ever I believe that whatever shall happen is best…. Would the complex forces which made a complex unit in Me resolve themselves backward into simpler forms or would my angel still be winging his way onward when eternities had passed? I could not tell—but all was doubtless well—and so with a "God forgive me if I'm wrong" I slept.

A sketch of one of the Union Army's medical tents on the site of the battle of Antietam Creek, Maryland, September 17, 1862. More than 17,000 men were wounded, Holmes among them. He was carried on a stretcher from the battlefield to a temporary hospital; he had been shot in the back of the neck, once again escaping serious injury.

given an opium pill for the pain, and three days later was able to begin his journey home to Boston.

Soon after Holmes rejoined the 20th Regiment after his second convalescence, it encountered some particularly heavy fighting in the Fredericksburg area of Virginia, where 165 of its soldiers were killed when caught in a Confederate ambush. Holmes, confined to a hospital some miles away with dysentery, had missed that skirmish. But on hearing the noise of firearms, he climbed a hill near the hospital and "saw the battle—a terrible sight when your Reg[iment] is in it but you are safe," as he wrote to his mother.

One of Holmes's Harvard classmates, Henry L. Abbott, had been a platoon leader in the Fredericksburg battle. Holmes heard reports of how Abbott calmly followed orders to move forward into the ambush, even though it amounted to almost certain death. Only a last-minute order stopping the advance saved Abbott. Later Abbott was killed in the bloody battle of Wilderness, where the Army of the Potomac lost more than 32,000 men. As he continued in the war, Holmes came to see what he called Abbott's "splendid carelessness of death" as a contrast to his own feelings. More and more he had begun to concentrate on his own survival rather than on the adventures he was having. At the same time he had begun to feel guilty about not sharing Abbott's bravery in the face of death.

In May 1863 Holmes received his third wound. It came when his regiment was engaged in another unsuccessful campaign to invade Richmond. Battles between the Union and Confederate forces were taking place in the Chancellorsville area of Virginia, north of Falmouth, where the 20th Regiment was stationed. Holmes's regiment was ordered to move north toward Fredericksburg, which lies between Falmouth and Chancellorsville, in order to attack the Confederates from the rear. When Holmes's regiment approached, the Confederate forces brought out a cannon and fired shots at the Union soldiers. Holmes's company was directly in the line of fire. One shot hit his knapsack, knocking it to pieces; the next hit him in the heel. He was given chloroform as a painkiller, and the cannon shot was extracted from his heel. Another journey to Boston, and another convalescence, lay ahead.

Although his heel injury was never life-threatening, Holmes required seven months to recover. During that time, he began to consider the possibility of taking a staff position, somewhat away from the front lines, and when he returned to active service in January 1864, it was as an aide to General Horatio Wright of the Sixth Corps. The cumulative horrors of the war were beginning to take their toll on Holmes. He wrote his mother in June 1864, after the terrible Chancellorsville and Wilderness campaigns had ended, that he was thinking of waiving promotion and leaving the service. "The reason," he said, was that "a doubt demoralizes me as it does any nervous man—and now I

This sketch of one of the battles around Chancellorsville, Virginia, May 5–12, 1864, shows the terrible carnage that resulted from Union and Confederate troops shooting rifles at each other from close range in densely wooded terrain. 30,000 Union soldiers were killed in area fighting, but Holmes—now an aide to a general instead of an infantryman—was out of the line of fire.

honestly think the duty of fighting has ceased for me." He meant that he could not put up with the constant threat of his own death anymore.

In July 1864 Holmes's three-year enlistment was to expire, and he resolved not to reenlist. Although he was offered a promotion to colonel, and an opportunity to return to his original regiment, Holmes wanted to leave, and he was formally discharged on July 17 in Petersburg, Virginia. Two days later he was back home in Boston, his wartime service concluded.

Holmes's experiences in the Civil War were to have a lasting influence on the rest of his life. He took from his Civil War service a realization of the gap between his romantic conception of war and his actual experience as a soldier. Nonetheless, in his later life, Holmes wrote essays glorifying the role of the soldier and suggesting that his generation had been privileged to have been "touched with fire," to have had the opportunity to participate firsthand in the war. One wonders whether these later portraits of his wartime service were efforts to convince himself of something worthwhile in an experience that had left him, at least initially, filled with self-doubt. As Holmes grew older, the Confederacy became a distant memory and representatives of Southern states began to play important roles in national politics. Looking back at the "special experience" of his wartime generation, Holmes decided to suppress his doubts—doubts about the connection between the horrors of battle, the cause for which he had fought, and his own courage—and concluded that war was a romance after all.

When Holmes died in 1935, at the age of 94, his safety-deposit box was opened and the contents of his house at 1726 Eye Street in Washington, D.C., were inventoried. Among his property were two items from the Civil War. One was a very small paper parcel, the size of one finger, in which were contained two musket balls. On the inside of the paper was written, in Holmes's hand, "These were taken from my body in the Civil War." The other item, found in his bedroom closet, was a pair of Civil War uniforms. Pinned on the uniforms was another note from Holmes: "These uniforms were worn by me in the Civil War and the stains upon them are my blood." Both memos conveyed the same message: Holmes had fought in the war, laid his life on the line, and survived. He wanted to be honored as a soldier.

Whaling ships in the Boston harbor in the late 1860s, with their numerous barrels of whale oil. The number of commercial ships in the Boston area led Holmes to develop a specialty in admiralty and maritime law, which deals with legal problems that occur on ships while they are in navigable waters, such as the loss of cargo during a voyage or accidents to seamen when a ship is moored in a harbor.

THE PRACTICAL STRUGGLE OF LIFE: BECOMING A LAWYER AND A JUDGE

"If I survive the war," Holmes had written in his autobiographical sketch for the 1861 Harvard class album, "I expect to study law as my profession or at least for a starting point." The phrase reflected more than a young person's uncertainty about the future. In 1861 many of Holmes's contemporaries simply studied law as "a starting point" to something else. It was common in the 18th and 19th centuries for men—not women—to study law as part of their general education. Law was an established profession by the time Wendell Holmes entered Harvard Law School in 1864, but it was also a gentlemanly pursuit.

The Boston to which Holmes returned in 1864, and which would serve as his home for the remainder of the 19th century, was already taking on signs of changing from a seaport town to an urban metropolis. As a boy Holmes had remembered being able to stand near his house and look out over the waterfront, where the constant activity of ships signaled that most commercial traffic in the area took place on water. Huge horse-chestnut trees lined the streets and the Boston Common, a grassy area of public land originally laid out in the 17th century. Public buildings were

A map of the Back Bay section of Boston in 1871, showing the new residential areas created by dredging up sand and filling in shallow portions of Boston Bay. The Back Bay, whose creation testified to the growth of Boston as a commercial center after the Civil War, became a prized housing location for affluent Bostonians, including Holmes's parents and, after their marriage in 1872, Wendell Holmes and Fanny Dixwell Holmes.

not much taller than private houses. The waters of Boston Bay extended far into Boston itself, linking up with the Charles River, so that most of the public buildings and houses were clustered on a peninsula surrounded by a bay and a river and overlooking the Atlantic Ocean.

By 1864 the railroad had come to Boston, making commercial and passenger transportation to the North, South, and West of the city much easier. Boston's population grew rapidly, and the Back Bay project, which consisted of filling in the shallow waters of Boston Bay to the west of the common, was underway. The Back Bay was to become a fashionable residential area, and the Holmes family was to build a house on Beacon Street in the Back Bay. By the beginning of the 1870s Wendell Holmes himself had taken an apartment in the Back Bay area. Bostonians now expected that their seagoing traffic would be connected to railroads and shipped all over the United States, that they would take streetcars as well as ride horseback or in carriages, and that they would live in a city with far more people, more noise, more traffic, bigger buildings, and more wealth than the

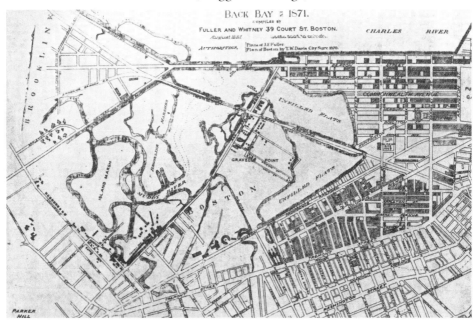

town into which Wendell had been born. It was that city in which Wendell Holmes was going to practice law.

To become a practicing lawyer in the United States in the 1860s, a person needed to do one of two things. Either he attached himself to an existing lawyer as an apprentice or he went to a law school near his home. He could usually attend the law school by simply signing up and going to lectures. After going to lectures, or "reading law," as it was called, for some time period, usually about two years, the aspiring lawyer was given an oral examination by a member of the local group of lawyers—called a "bar" and normally associated with a city or county—to see if he had a general understanding of legal subjects, such as criminal law, personal property, contracts, civil injuries, and admiralty or maritime law.

Those oral examinations were not particularly extensive or difficult, and it was not necessary to have a degree from a law school in order to take the exams and practice law. Holmes entered the legal profession in Massachusetts in March 1867, but he had taken classes at Harvard Law School only from September 1864 through December 1865. After that he had attached himself to a Boston law office and began "looking up cases" as an apprentice. In June 1866 he received his Harvard LL.B., then took the rest of the summer off to travel in Europe. Holmes returned to Boston as an apprentice in the fall and took his oral bar examination in March 1867. After passing it, he went to work for the law firm where he had been an apprentice. This experience was typical for lawyers in Holmes's day who had chosen to go to law school.

The Harvard Law School that Holmes entered in 1864 was very different, both in the method of instruction and the demands on its students, from modern law schools. The courses were not taught through conversations between professors and students about the details of cases, as most first-year law courses are today. Instead, they consisted of

Dane Hall, the sole building in which Harvard Law School was housed from 1832, when it was built, until 1883, when an additional building was constructed. This sketch, made in 1850, shows Dane Hall in the same condition it would have been in 1864, when Holmes Jr. first attended law lectures.

lectures by the professors, based on textbooks they or others had written, followed by oral quizzes testing the students' grasp of the material. Attendance at class was not required, and the students received no grades. The only requirement for admission was a certificate of good character—one could enter Harvard Law School without a college degree—and the only requirement for graduation was one and a half years of registration at the law school. There were no written examinations at all, so that the only thing that a degree from Harvard meant was that a student had signed up for classes for at least three semesters. Three professors made up the entire law school faculty.

In 1870, when Holmes was practicing law in Boston and writing essays for *The American Law Review,* Harvard Law School decided to require each of its graduating students to pass a written examination. In an unsigned editorial in that journal, Holmes applauded this change. In his opinion, "A school which undertook to confer degrees without any preliminary examination ... was doing something ... to injure the profession throughout the country, and to discourage real students."

In addition to his dissatisfaction with Harvard Law School, Holmes discovered that the legal profession itself did not necessarily appeal to him in his 20s. Later in his life he described his first encounters with legal study: "When I began, the law presented itself as a ragbag of details.... It was not without anguish that one asked oneself whether the subject was worthy of the interest of an intelligent man. One saw people who one respected and admired leaving the study because they thought it narrowed the mind." In the spring of 1865 Holmes entered into a correspondence with Henry Brownell, a poet whose writings about the Civil War had attracted him. "Truth sifts so slowly from the dust of the law," he told Brownell, mentioning that he found both poetry and philosophy more stimulating. A "danger" about law study, he confessed to Brownell, was that one was so easily distracted from it. "It is so easy and pleasant," he continued, "to go from day to day satisfying yourself for not having knocked off a hundred pages of Evidence or Contracts," but rather "having turned over a few stones in some new mind ... or [having] read some new poem or (worse) written one."

But in that same letter Holmes said to Brownell that "my first year at law satisfies me." By the fall of 1865 his reaction was more favorable. He described law to Brownell as "my enthusiastic pursuit" and said that he now understood "how men come to prefer a professional to a general reputation—and for the sake of the former ... will sacrifice every hope of the other." The satisfaction in a professional reputation, he had come to believe, came from mastery of one's specialized subject, which one achieved by immersing oneself in details. Over the next several years, Holmes served as a coeditor of *The American Law Review,* devoted to legal topics; edited the 12th edition of James Kent's *Commentaries on American Law,* a well-known legal source-book; gave a course of lectures on jurisprudence at Harvard College in the spring of 1872; and from 1867 on, wrote a series of book reviews, digests of legal decisions, and scholarly articles for *The American Law Review.*

As Holmes continued on in his absorbed pursuit of his chosen profession, he demonstrated an extraordinary capacity to "get to the bottom," as he put it, of legal issues. This capacity for hard work and hard thought eventually made Holmes realize that in concentrating on the law, he was not necessarily giving up his earlier love of philosophy. "I have learned, after a laborious and somewhat painful period of probation," he wrote in 1876 to the poet and essayist Ralph Waldo Emerson, one of his heroes as a Harvard undergraduate, "that the law opens a way to philosophy as well as anything else."

Holmes's first full-time exposure to law practice had been in 1866 as an apprentice with the firm of George Shattuck, an experienced trial lawyer 12 years older than Holmes. After passing the bar, Holmes officially joined the Shattuck firm. Shattuck had a general practice, representing merchants, shipowners, and importers and exporters engaged in maritime commerce; businessmen; individuals participating in real estate transactions; fire insurance companies; and banks. He was not as intellectually inclined as Holmes, but he was quick on his feet, shrewd, and impressive in court. Holmes began his career doing office work, which consisted of drafting contracts for clients. Gradually, as Shattuck's practice grew and Holmes gained more experience, Holmes began to try cases in court himself, making a specialty of admiralty cases.

Admiralty is the body of law that involves cases dealing with the high seas or the "navigable waters of the United States." What is called a "navigable water" is sometimes disputed, and admiralty lawyers need to learn the technicalities of the field, which has its own rules. For example, when a ship is injured in dry dock, the legal rules for compensating the owner for that injury may be different from the rules governing injury when a ship collides with another leaving port. The dry dock injury may not be governed by admiralty rules, but the collision injury would be. After several years Holmes understood the technicalities of admiralty law well and regularly appeared in court to represent shipowners.

By the early 1870s Holmes had become an established lawyer with the Shattuck firm. But he did not seem satisfied, as Shattuck was, with devoting all his professional energies to the practice of law. He continued to write articles for *The American Law Review* and in 1870 became sole editor of that journal. A sense of the intensity of his professional pursuits can be gathered from an entry he wrote in one of his journals for June 17, 1872. (Holmes began keeping journals in 1866; in them he compiled lists of his reading and wrote occasional comments on his other activities, including his travels.) The June 17 entry contained the line "Married. Sole editor of Am. L. Rev." That and another entry indicating that "Fanny read proof" of his Kent edition were the only mention of the fact that after more than 20 years of friendship Wendell Holmes and Fanny Bowditch Dixwell had married one another. She was the daughter of Epes Sergant Dixwell, headmaster of the private school Holmes had attended between the ages of 10 and 16, when he entered Harvard.

Despite the offhand reference Holmes made to his marriage, his relationship with Fanny was one of the defining events of his life. From the time Wendell entered Harvard in 1857, he considered Fanny a close friend and corresponded with her during his service in the Civil War. After his return from the war in 1864, they were regular social companions, and their friends and families expected them eventually to marry.

They did not become engaged, however, until 1872. Financial reasons may have delayed their marriage. Holmes's family was not particularly wealthy (most of the family money would eventually come from the royalties on Holmes Sr.'s writings), and Fanny's family was of quite modest means. But Holmes Sr. also confessed a concern that his son did not seem to be inclined to make a commitment to Fanny. He believed that his son was too preoccupied with his career, but there was some evidence that Wendell was preoccupied with other young women as well.

In some respects Fanny Dixwell and Wendell Holmes were opposites. He liked socializing, exchanging ideas, and flirting with women. She was a relatively solitary person who grew more reclusive as she aged. A month after her marriage, Fanny had a severe attack of rheumatic fever (a

Fanny Bowditch Dixwell with her siblings, taken in the 1860s, when she was in her 20s. Wendell and Fanny first met in 1851, when Wendell enrolled in a private school taught by Epes Sargent Dixwell, Fanny's father. By the time Wendell had graduated from Harvard, they were romantically linked, although they did not marry until 1872, when Fanny was 32 and Wendell 31.

bacterial infection, now treatable with antibiotics) and was bedridden for several months. (Many years later, in 1895, she suffered a second attack.) At the time of the marriage, Wendell was preoccupied with his law practice and his legal writings. His immersion in work and Fanny's illness established themes that would endure throughout the marriage. Fanny remained concerned largely with solitary, domestic tasks and Wendell used his leisure time to socialize, often without Fanny's company. He once said of Fanny, "She is a very solitary bird, and if her notion of duty did not compel her to do otherwise, she would be an absolute recluse, I think…. She and I are a queer contrast in that way, as in many others."

Fanny may have been solitary, but she was not dull. She and Wendell traveled to Europe in 1874, and Fanny kept a diary in which she made satiric comments about their fellow passengers on the ship and during their time in London. She produced needlework embroideries of such a high quality that they were exhibited in museums in Boston and New York in 1880 and 1881 and reviewed in newspapers. She liked to tease her husband and play practical jokes on him. When Holmes was a justice of the U.S. Supreme Court, Fanny once conspired with Holmes's law clerk to place a fake cockroach on the top of a barrel of flour kept in the basement of the Holmes' house. She then pretended to be afraid of the cockroach and asked for Holmes's help. When he squirmed, she noted that it was April Fool's Day. Fanny also managed the Holmes's domestic finances, and in 1888, after Wendell's mother and younger sister had both died within a two-year span, she took over the management of Holmes Sr.'s household for the remaining six years of his life. When she died, Wendell wrote a friend that "for over fifty years [of marriage] she made life poetry for me."

After their marriage in 1872, Wendell and Fanny took up residence in an apartment in Boston, near Wendell's parents, and Holmes continued to pursue his goals in the legal profession. He was interested in becoming, within the law, as famous as his father had become in the worlds of medicine and literature. He wanted to gain recognition for his scholarship, and he hoped eventually to become a judge.

Becoming a judge is partly a matter of how good a lawyer one is and partly a matter of politics. From the time that the United States came into existence, politicians have been interested in playing a role in the appointment of judges. They understand how important the law is as a source of authority. Judges are responsible for deciding what the laws mean in a particular legal dispute. So politicians have a strong interest in helping select officials who will, they hope, agree with them about most issues. In some states, however, judges are elected to office, although they do not campaign in the same way as politicians because they are expected to be impartial and not bound to any particular party. All federal judges and many state judges are appointed by politicians rather than elected.

In the state of Massachusetts, at the time when Holmes was a young lawyer in Boston, there were three kinds of judgeships, all of which were appointive rather than elective offices. The first two judgeships had been created by the state's constitution, and the third by the Constitution of the United States. The first level of state judgeships was composed of state trial judges, who presided over ordinary legal disputes, such as highway or railroad accidents, crimes, divorces and custody disputes, and arguments about the ownership of property or the meaning of contracts between people in business relationships. Massachusetts was divided into counties, and each county had its own trial court. Trial judges were usually appointed by the state legislature. But trial judgeships were almost always filled by lawyers who had practiced in the county where the trial court was located. So it was important that lawyers who wanted to be considered for judgeships have good reputations among their fellow county practitioners.

The second level of state judgeships was composed of the justices on the Supreme Judicial Court of Massachusetts. That court's main purpose was to hear appeals from the state trial courts. There were seven judges of that court when Holmes was practicing law, and they were appointed by the governor of the state. Their decisions were made as a group: When a trial court case was appealed, either they voted to uphold the decision of the trial court or they reversed it and entered their own decision. Most of the decisions of the Supreme Judicial Court were unanimous, though not all. The position supported by a majority of the justices was the final resolution of the case on appeal.

The third type of judgeship in Massachusetts was known as a federal district judgeship. Federal courts were expected to hear legal disputes between citizens of different states, disputes in which the federal government was involved, or disputes involving the high seas or waterways that crossed state lines. Congress had established federal courts so that different states, or citizens from different states, might not be put at a disadvantage by having their case heard in another state. If a citizen of Massachusetts were run down in New Hampshire by a New Hampshire company's milk wagon, for example, the Massachusetts citizen might think that a New Hampshire trial court would be inclined to side with the position of a local company rather than a stranger from another state. The federal courts were available for such suits.

The federal trial courts were called district courts, named for the districts in which they sat. Congress decided the size and number of federal districts: In late-19th-century Massachusetts there were state trial courts for every county but only two federal district courts in the entire state. Federal district judges moved around within their district, holding court in county courthouses in some areas. In larger cities, such as Boston, the federal district court had its own courthouse.

Federal district courts were important in the 19th century because a number of their cases could be appealed directly to the Supreme Court of the United States. This was not true of state trial courts: Their cases needed to be decided by the highest court in a state (such as the Supreme Judicial Court of Massachusetts) before they could be appealed, and there were limitations even on appeals from the highest state courts. As a result, when large sums of money or interesting points of law were at stake, people who were able to bring their cases before a federal district court often did so. The job of a federal district judge was a stimulating and prestigious one.

In 1878, after Holmes had been practicing law for nearly 13 years, his name was mentioned by fellow lawyers in Boston in connection with a federal district judgeship vacancy there. One of the reasons Holmes was considered had to do with the kind of law that he practiced. Admiralty law was particularly important in Boston because a great deal of its commerce and passenger traffic was still on ships, and Boston was one of the country's leading ports and shipping centers. Holmes represented shipowners in their claims against insurance companies and defended them against a variety of suits by seamen or passengers for injuries or unpaid wages; he also represented insurance companies that sought to avoid payment of those claims and merchants whose cargo had been damaged or lost on a voyage.

The U.S. Constitution provides that all cases on the high seas and in navigable waters within the United States can be brought in federal district courts. Boston lawyers whose practice included admiralty cases often appeared in those courts. When the federal district judgeship in Boston became vacant in 1878, Holmes's old friend John Gray, who had also fought in the Civil War and was practicing in Boston and teaching at Harvard Law School, wrote a letter to the attorney general of the United States recommending Holmes because of his expertise in admiralty law. Another of his lawyer friends in Boston officially recommended Holmes as well. For a while it appeared that Holmes would be appointed, because the President of the United States, Rutherford Hayes, believed that he and Holmes, who had both fought for the Army of the Potomac in the Civil War, had been wounded in the same battle.

Appointments to federal district judgeships are made by the President, usually on the recommendation of the attorney general, but the President also typically consults the senators of the states in which the vacancies exist. President Hayes asked Senator George Frisbee Hoar, the senior senator from Massachusetts, what he thought of Holmes. Hoar did not admire Holmes and recommended another Boston lawyer, whom Hayes agreed to nominate. So Holmes, at the age of 37, remained in the practice of law. On first hearing of the possibility of his appointment, Holmes had written a friend that although "the place is not desirable for the money … it would enable me to work in the way I want to and so I should like it." His disappointment on not receiving the position did not cause Holmes to abandon his hopes of eventually securing a judgeship. Senator Hoar, however, remained determined to prevent that from happening.

At the time when the district judgeship possibility emerged, Holmes was at one of the busiest stages of his career. In addition to his active law practice, he was continuing to write articles—now primarily on legal history and jurisprudence (philosophy of law)— for *The American Law Review* steadily from 1876 through 1880. He wrote to other legal scholars that he was planning to make a book out of those articles, what he called "a

U.S. Senator George Frisbie Hoar, Massachusetts' senior senator when Holmes was considered for a federal district judgeship (1878) and nominated to the Supreme Court (1902). Hoar opposed Holmes's candidacy both times, regarding him as an unpredictable man who lacked solid judgment.

new First Book of the Law," which would set forth "the fundamental ... principles of our substantive law." (By "substantive law" Holmes meant the rules of law laid down in cases involving contract disputes, crimes, domestic quarrels, and other ordinary cases.)

In 1879 Holmes received an opportunity to create that book. He was invited to give a course of lectures on common law by the Lowell Institute, which sponsored public lectures in the Boston area. ("Common law" is the term for the entire body of judicial decisions in England and America, stretching back many centuries, that forms the basis of the legal rules that are applied to ordinary court cases.) Holmes worked for most of the calendar year of 1880 on the 12 lectures, which he delivered in November and December. Some were modified versions of his articles; others were written for the occasion. Holmes delivered each lecture without notes, although the subject matter was quite technical and depended on precise language. The lectures were eventually published in March 1881 as a book entitled *The Common Law.*

The Common Law is still in print. It is very likely the best-known book ever written about American law. But it is a difficult, sometimes obscure book, which today's lawyers and law students find largely inaccessible. Nonetheless it remains one of the most important and original books on law written by an American, and it contains some passages that are frequently quoted today, such as this one from the opening paragraph:

> The life of the law has not been logic: It has been experience. The felt necessities of the time, the prevalent moral and political theories, intuitions of public policy, avowed or unconscious, even the prejudices which judges share with their fellowmen, have had a good deal more to do than the syllogism [a formula of logical reasoning] in determining the rules by which men should be governed.

Holmes's general point in that paragraph may seem an obvious one today, when people expect that law will closely track the beliefs and experiences of those who make legal decisions. It was, however, an unusual and controversial claim in 1881. In those days most legal scholars and judges thought of judging as a rigorous logical process of finding preexisting legal rules and applying them to the facts of cases—similar to the way a mathematician might apply axioms to solve geometry problems. People did not think the process of judging involved much creativity, or awareness of the surrounding context of cases, or recognition of the political consequences of a decision. Holmes suggested that judging involved all those elements and that the judicial use of "logic" served to conceal them.

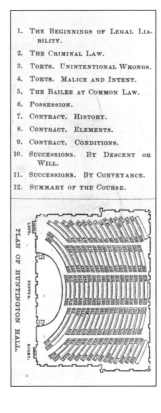

A ticket to the 12 lectures on "The Common Law," delivered by Holmes at the Lowell Institute in Boston in November and December 1880 on successive Tuesday and Friday evenings. Holmes had memorized the text of all 12 lectures and delivered them without consulting any notes.

There were several people in the audience for Holmes's Lowell lectures who were impressed with Holmes's mastery of his subjects and his original, provocative views on the role of "experience" and "logic" in law. Among them included some members of the Harvard law faculty, which consisted, at the time, of four professors, including John Gray and another longtime acquaintance, James Bradley Thayer, with whom Holmes had worked in law practice between 1866 and 1871. Shortly after *The Common Law* was published, Holmes received an offer to join the Harvard law faculty.

Sometime in the fall of 1881, Charles W. Eliot, the president of Harvard University, approached Holmes and asked if he would be interested in accepting a new professorship on the law faculty. Eliot apparently believed that the money for the professorship had been secured, and he and Holmes began to discuss the terms of the offer. On November 1, 1881, Holmes wrote to Eliot that he was ready to accept a professorship at Harvard Law School if certain "terms" were "satisfactory." He mentioned the salary, which would be $5,000 a year, the opportunity for him to "devote a reasonable proportion of my time … to studies touching the history and philosophy of law," and an expectation that if the salaries of other professors at Harvard were raised, his would be as well. Then Holmes added a last condition: "If a judgeship should be offered me I should not wish to feel bound in honor not to consider it, although I do not know that I should take it and although my present acceptance will diminish the chance of

A picture of Holmes taken by Clover Hooper, the wife of historian and essayist Henry Adams, in the early 1880s. Around this time Holmes had joined the Harvard Law School faculty then resigned suddenly to become associate justice of the Supreme Judicial Court of Massachusetts.

such an offer and is for that reason against the advice of many of my friends."

Eliot responded by saying that all of Holmes's terms were satisfactory. Holmes prepared to accept the professorship, but then it turned out that the funding for it had not been secured. When Holmes learned of this, he decided to withdraw his acceptance, feeling that now any fund-raising efforts for the professorship would amount to a favor to him.

But James Bradley Thayer believed that money for a professorship could be raised without its being designated for Holmes, and in January 1882, he began contacting possible donors. He quickly came up with one, William Weld, who was still in the process of receiving his degree at Harvard Law School. Weld had inherited more than $3 million from his grandfather, a very large sum at the time, and he offered $90,000 for the new professorship. More money than the cost of the professor's salary is always needed so that the endowment—the rest of the money—can be invested and grow over the years. Holmes became the William Weld Professor of Jurisprudence in February 1882, and $5,000 of the $90,000 endowment was used to pay his first year's salary.

Holmes was not expected to begin teaching courses until the fall of that year, but he attended faculty meetings in March and May and began preparing his courses. He was expected to offer five separate courses over the course of the 1882–83 academic year.

In September 1882 Holmes began his career as a full-time law professor. Three months later, that career suddenly came to a close. Holmes resigned his professorship to accept the position of associate justice on the Supreme Judicial Court of Massachusetts. The circumstances of Holmes's departure shocked and angered his colleagues on the Harvard faculty.

On Friday, December 8, 1882, Holmes was having lunch with Professor James Barr Ames in Cambridge when

Fanny Holmes and George Shattuck arrived in a carriage. Shattuck told Holmes that about an hour ago, Governor John Long had told him that he intended to appoint Holmes to a vacant judgeship on the Supreme Judicial Court, but that Holmes needed to make an immediate decision on whether he would accept. The time pressure was because Long had only three weeks left as governor. All judicial nominations made by the governor had to be considered by a committee known as the Governor's Council for at least one week, and that council had its last scheduled meeting that very afternoon, at three o'clock.

Holmes immediately got into the carriage with Fanny and Shattuck, drove to Governor Long's office, and accepted the appointment as judge. His name was given to the Governor's Council that afternoon, and the next day the Boston papers announced his appointment. Holmes had not told any of the other professors at Harvard Law School, or President Eliot, that he had been offered a judgeship, let alone that he had accepted it.

The first communication Holmes had with his colleagues was at a faculty meeting on December 12. After that meeting Thayer reported in his journal that Holmes had "made a long, excited and wholly ineffective attempt to account for his [accepting the judgeship]," but that no one on the law faculty "said a word, *not one*." Holmes then left the meeting, seeming, in Thayer's view, "to have no sense of any impropriety in what he had done."

Subsequently Holmes let it be known about the terms he had agreed to with Eliot on accepting the professorship, calling attention to his request to be free to accept a judgeship. This excuse was not satisfactory to Thayer. "It cannot be denied that Holmes was within the line of his legal right," Thayer wrote in his journal. "But what shall be said of his sense of what is morally admissible—of his sense of honor, of justice, of consideration of the rights of others and their sensibilities, when he could do what he did."

Holmes gave some reasons later in his life about why he wanted so badly to be a judge. He said that Fanny told him he had "grown sober with an inherent sense of limitation" after accepting the offer to teach at Harvard. By that, he explained, he meant that "the law ... is a limited subject" and that he had already written a book in which he had sought to set out the philosophical foundations and to explore the history of the U.S. legal system. He was not sure he had anything more to say. He might spend the rest of his scholarly life repeating the insights of *The Common Law* or perhaps going into a new field. If he chose the latter course, he said, he was not sure how long his mind would remain "suggestive," by which he meant capable of generating original ideas.

Two indirect comments he made in letters, however, perhaps come closer to providing an explanation for his desire to be a judge. Explaining that he had left Harvard for a judgeship, Holmes wrote to a friend: "I did not think one could without moral loss decline any share in the practical struggle of life which naturally offered itself and for which he believed himself fitted.... I felt that if I declined the struggle offered me I should never be so happy again—I should feel that I had chosen the less manly course." In a second letter, written to his young friend Felix Frankfurter after Frankfurter had received an offer to teach at Harvard Law School in 1913, Holmes said something quite similar. "Academic life," he wrote Frankfurter,

> is but half life—it is withdrawal from the fight in order to utter smart things that cost you nothing except the thinking them from a cloister.... Business in the world is unhappy, often seems mean, and always challenges your power to idealize the brute fact—but it hardens the fibre and I think is more likely to make more of a man of one who turns it to success.

For Holmes judging had enough of life's ordinary details, and enough direct consequences for the humans whose disputes came before courts, to qualify as the equivalent of the business world. One of the most intellectually oriented of U.S. judges, a man who instinctively gravitated—whether as a lawyer, legal scholar, law professor, or judge—to the realm of legal philosophy, where abstract thought predominated, derived much of his professional self-esteem from the feeling that he was engaged in the practical struggle of life.

"THE LIFE OF THE LAW HAS NOT BEEN LOGIC"

The Common Law *appeared originally in March 1881 and is still in print. Holmes's object in the book was to discuss the "history and existing theories of legislation" surrounding legal subjects such as crimes, torts, contracts, and property transactions. By "theories of legislation" Holmes meant the policy reasons for preferring one legal rule over another in those subjects. The book's opening paragraph, especially the sentence "The life of the law has not been logic: it has been experience," is one of the most famous in American legal literature.*

The object of this book is to present a general view of the Common Law. To accomplish this task, other tools are needed besides logic. It is something to show that the consistency of a system requires a particular result, but it is not all. The life of the law has not been logic: it has been experience. The felt necessities of the time, the prevalent moral and political theories, intuitions of public policy, avowed or unconscious, even the prejudices which judges share with their fellow-men, have had a good deal more to do than the syllogism in determining the rules by which men should be governed. The law embodies the story of a nation's development through many centuries, and it cannot be dealt with as if it contained only the axioms and corollaries of a book of mathematics. In order to know what it is, we must know what it has been, and what it tends to become. We must alternately consult history and existing theories of legislation. But the most difficult labor will be to understand the combination of the two into new products at every stage. The substance of the law at any given time pretty nearly corresponds, so far as it goes, with what is then understood to be convenient; but its form and machinery, and the degree to which it is able to work out desired results, depend very much on its past.

The Suffolk County (Boston) courthouse, built in 1893, where Holmes and his fellow judges on the Supreme Judicial Court of Massachusetts heard arguments and made decisions in cases that were appealed to them from trial courts all over the state. The Supreme Judicial Court met here fall through spring; during the summer months some of the justices, on a rotating basis, were required to preside over trial courts in various locations, while others were excused from judicial responsibilities.

4

THE QUIET YEARS

If anyone had been making predictions about Holmes's career as a judge, he or she might have been inclined to predict that Holmes's 20 years on the Supreme Judicial Court of Massachusetts would be the pivotal chapter in his judicial life. During these years Holmes was in the prime of life for a man of his time: He was appointed at the age of 41 and remained on the court past his 61st birthday. Although many judges are appointed for life, and thus do not face mandatory retirement, most of them, even today, do not continue on a full-time basis beyond the age of 70. By 1902, when Holmes joined the Supreme Court of the United States, he had served as chief justice of the Supreme Judicial Court of Massachusetts for three years and was the most senior judge, both in terms of age and in terms of service, on that court.

Holmes's experience on the Supreme Judicial Court of Massachusetts, however, had not been as memorable, at least in the sense of widening his professional reputation, as he had probably expected. Nor had he had the opportunity to put into practice the ideas about common law subjects he had developed as a scholar. It had been, in the eyes of the general public, a quiet time. Holmes was nearly as obscure to most Americans in 1902 as he had been in 1882. It had also been a quiet time in terms of Holmes's professional routine. The Supreme Judicial Court discouraged public attention to the individual opinions of judges and emphasized instead the court's collective decisions.

To an extent Holmes, who had always thirsted for public recognition and who had become a judge hoping to wield considerable public influence, was disappointed with the relatively anonymous and sometimes humdrum nature of his judicial work. He found that he could do his job as a judge, which consisted of listening to cases in court, conferring with the other judges on the Supreme Court of Massachusetts, and writing opinions deciding cases, quite quickly and easily. To occupy himself he began to accept speaking invitations and write scholarly articles, and he published a volume of his speeches privately in 1891. He also enjoyed Boston social life, increasingly without the company of Fanny, who preferred to remain at home. Many of his social contacts were with women, and he developed a reputation as a flirt.

Despite his numerous female friendships and Fanny's reclusiveness, Holmes did not become romantically involved with other women during his years on the Supreme Judicial Court of Massachusetts, with one exception. As early as 1866, before his marriage, he had traveled in England, and he returned there with Fanny in 1874 and 1882. In 1889, however, after his mother's and sister's deaths, Fanny urged him to go alone while she took over the organization of his father's household. Wendell went, stayed for three months, and enjoyed an active social life. During that summer he met the wife of an Irish member of Parliament, Clare Castletown, at a party. In 1891, when his book of speeches appeared, he sent Clare Castletown a copy, and she responded with a thank-you note inviting him to look her and her husband up on his next visit to England.

That visit came in 1896, when Holmes again traveled without Fanny. He not only renewed acquaintance with Clare Castletown, he spent a good deal of time in her company, both in London and on her estate, Doneraile Court, in south central Ireland. After two weeks at Doneraile Court, in August 1896, where Clare entertained him and other guests in the absence of her husband, Holmes became infatuated with Clare. For the next two years he wrote her a series of letters that one historian has accurately described as

An unsigned, unidentified photograph found in Holmes's papers after his death. In 1896 Clare Castletown, 41, sent him a picture of herself. A painting of Clare Castletown in one of her estates, Doneraile Court near Mallow, Ireland, bears a striking resemblance to this portrait.

"love letters," although the letters do not suggest that Holmes and Clare had a physical relationship. Nonetheless it was clear that he was emotionally involved with Clare Castletown—in one letter he said "I love, love, love you and think, think, think about you"—and it is also clear that Clare encouraged Wendell's feelings, although neither seemed to think of the relationship as a threat to their marriages. After 1899, when Clare temporarily left Ireland to join her husband in the Boer War in South Africa, and especially after 1902, when Holmes left Boston to join the U.S. Supreme Court in Washington, the relationship between Clare and Wendell diminished in intensity. But it was a symbol of Holmes's restlessness in the years of his service on the Supreme Judicial Court of Massachusetts, and perhaps also a symbol of the separate lives that he and Fanny had come to lead.

Holmes's restlessness as a judge on the Supreme Judicial Court of Massachusetts was not, however, the only response that job engendered in him. In a letter to Clare, he wrote that he did his judicial work in a "kind of bitter loneliness," alluding to his sense of anonymity and lack of recognition. In the same letter, however, he spoke of judging as bringing him "great joy."

A 1900 speech Holmes made to the Bar Association of Boston, after he had become the chief justice of the Supreme Judicial Court, captured his attitude in the quiet professional years of his life. At one point in the speech he said that when he reflected on his career as a judge, he found that he had written opinions in about 1,000 cases. Many of those cases, he felt, were "on trifling or transitory matters." He would have preferred "to study to the bottom and to say his say on every question which the law has ever presented ... and then to generalize it all and write it in continuous, logical, philosophic exposition." But instead he had directed his energies toward deciding a great many cases of comparatively little significance. "Alas, gentlemen, that is life," he concluded. "We cannot live our dreams."

In the same speech, however, Holmes emphasized the "pleasure" of judging, "the pure pleasure of doing the work, irrespective of future aims," of putting "out one's power in some ... useful or harmless way."

In these comments Holmes sounded as if he found judging boring or had resigned himself to the fact that judging was not the grand exercise he had imagined it would be. Actually, however, Holmes believed he had learned an important lesson from his experience as a Massachusetts judge. The lesson was that most legal cases were not all that important, either in their significance or intellectual challenges. But this did not make the job of judging insignificant. Judging was something more modest than Holmes had imagined but at the same time more real and more fundamental: Deciding cases did make a difference in people's lives. It was an obscure job but still an important one.

Most of the cases that came before the Supreme Judicial Court of Massachusetts were not complicated ones, and they did not raise difficult questions of law that required sustained and serious thought. Most of the cases did not ask a judge to "study them to the bottom." And even the few cases that were difficult, and threatened to produce differing opinions among the judges, could be reduced to simple choices on matters of policy. A judge in such a case exercised what Holmes called "the sovereign prerogative of choice," concluding that one policy was to be furthered at the expense of another.

In one of his opinions Holmes discussed the choices judges made. The case was a suit brought by the owner of a horse that had become frightened when it passed near a railroad track on which there was a freight train car with a flat surface and no top. An electric streetcar was resting on the train car, waiting to be unloaded. The streetcar was covered with a white canvas tarpaulin to protect it. Normally the railroad track was separated from the highway by an eight-foot fence, but that fence had been taken down to make moving the streetcar easier. When the horse saw the large canvas tarpaulin covering the streetcar, it was disturbed by the sight, bolted, and injured itself in the process.

The horse's owner sued the railroad for the horse's injuries, claiming that by taking down the fence and allowing the streetcar to remain in sight of horses on the high-

In late-19th-century cities various forms of transportation competed for space: railroads, streetcars, bicycles, and horse-drawn vehicles. Narrow and unpaved or cobblestone streets created hectic traffic conditions. Sometimes this scared horses, causing injury to them or their passengers.

way, the railroad had been negligent, or legally careless. The railroad defended itself on the ground that it could not carry certain types of freight unless it was permitted to carry it in open cars and to temporarily allow access to those cars from public highways. Holmes, in finding that the railroad had not been negligent, said:

> As in many cases, perhaps it might be said in all, two principles ... present themselves, each of which it would be desirable to carry out but for the other, but which at this point come into conflict. It is desirable that as far as possible people should be able to drive in the streets without their horses being frightened. It is also desirable ... that a railroad company should be free to use its tracks in any otherwise lawful way for the ... keeping and final delivery of any lawful freight. A line has to be drawn to separate the domains of the irreconcilable desires.

Drawing that line, Holmes felt, amounted to a policy choice. "Some uses of land might be imagined which would be held unlawful solely because of their tendency to frighten horses.... Others would be held lawful no matter how many horses they frightened." In the case before him the burdens on railroads appeared quite significant if they were prevented from covering freight with canvases that might frighten horses or from temporarily dismantling barriers between their tracks and public highways that might have the same effect. The burdens on horse owners resulting from Holmes's decision—they took the risk of injury to their horses if they drove them near railroad tracks when barriers separating those tracks from public highways were temporarily removed to move freight—appeared much less significant. But in the end the case turned on how a judge, or a group of judges, felt about burdening railroads shipping freight versus burdening people driving horses.

So there was nothing about the legal principle of negligence in the horse case that automatically decided the dispute. One could think of both the railroad and the horse owner as being careless, or one could think that neither one had been careless because the circumstances of the accident were quite unusual. So the decision in the case depended on whether, as a matter of social policy, a judge wanted to put the costs of injuries suffered by frightened horses on their owners or on railroads. If the case had involved a railroad car carrying wild animals being shipped to a zoo, and if the animals had broken loose from the car while it was resting on a track, passed onto the public highway because a barrier had been temporarily removed, and injured a passerby on that highway, the railroad would probably have been found negligent. But the decision to rule in favor of the injured passerby would still have been a policy choice.

The case of the frightened horse was one of the more complicated cases that Holmes encountered on the Supreme Judicial Court of Massachusetts. Most of his cases were simple appeals from the trial courts scattered around the state. A trial judge had decided a case; the losing party, not wanting to comply with the decision, had appealed on the ground that the judge had misunderstood or misapplied the law. Holmes and his fellow judges on the Supreme Judicial Court usually upheld the trial court because the questions of law at stake were relatively one-sided and the trial judge had in most cases decided those questions correctly. Most such cases were "trifling," not involving complicated matters or large amounts of money, and "transitory," not laying down any important or enduring legal principles.

Even if the cases Holmes encountered were insignificant, his job on the Supreme Judicial Court was not. Holmes and his colleagues were the final decision makers in legal disputes. When they made a decision, the case was over. One party had won and another had lost; someone went to jail or did not; money supposedly owed was paid or was not; one person or another bore the cost of an accident; property changed hands or did not. Not only did the judges have the power to make decisions that affected other people's lives—and, in most cases decided by Holmes and his colleagues, the power to make decisions that could not be appealed to any other authority—they had the power to decide questions of social policy as well as questions of law. Not a great many important policy questions came to Holmes on the Supreme Judicial Court of Massachusetts, but when they did, he and his fellow judges had the power to decide them.

But the fact that Holmes had a great deal of power did not necessarily mean that he had a great deal of recognition. He had been highly aware of the fame his father had secured through his writing and lecturing, and although he had quite consciously chosen not to be "popular" in the same way, he had written his scholarly essays, produced his edition of Kent's *Commentaries,* and published *The Common Law* in order to gain some recognition in legal circles. He certainly hoped that becoming a judge would provide him with opportunities to gain still more recognition, but once he joined the court he did not encounter many chances to put his mark on the cases he decided.

Holmes did not gain much individual recognition on the Supreme Judicial Court of Massachusetts because the court issued as many unanimous decisions as possible. In such decisions all seven judges on the court agreed with the position of the judge who wrote the opinion accompanying the decision, and the opinion was described as "the opinion of the court."

The practice of unanimous decisions was encouraged by the Supreme Judicial Court during Holmes's time on it—and is encouraged by all such courts today—because of what a decision of the highest court of a state represents. That decision is the final resolution of a dispute between two parties, but it is also an answer to any questions of law that arose in the course of the dispute. The answer the court gives to such questions will affect not only those involved in the case but many other people in the state. In the frightened horse case, Holmes's decision meant not only that the railroad did not have to pay for the damage the horse suffered but also that in the future railroads could unload freight near public highways even if their actions startled horses.

In cases in which the judges do not all agree, some judges write what are called dissenting opinions. Such opinions provide answers to the questions of law that are different from the opinion of the court, which is then called a majority opinion instead of a unanimous opinion. When this happens and the rules of law that emerge from the case are laid down by a majority, but not all, of the judges, the general public may not be quite as sure about whether the rules are good ones, even though they must be followed.

If one main purpose of the legal system is to establish rules that help guide the conduct of ordinary people, public uncertainty about the meaning of those rules and public difficulty in predicting whether the rules will apply to cases in the future are barriers to citizens' efforts to plan their conduct in accordance with the law. So, on the whole, the highest state courts prefer to issue just one opinion accompanying their decisions, the opinion of the court.

The issuance of a unanimous opinion of the court has one negative side effect, from the point of view of some judges. Unanimous opinions make it much more difficult for members of the public to recognize the individual contributions of judges. The practice of issuing unanimous opinions means that an individual judge will get to write an opinion only in one of five, seven, or nine cases, depending on how many judges sit on the court. In Holmes's case, in six out of seven cases decided by the Supreme Judicial Court of Massachusetts, he would very likely join a unanimous opinion written by another judge with whom he served; his own name would not even appear on that opinion. Not only would readers of the opinion learn nothing about Holmes's reasoning on the questions of law at stake in the case, but they might not even know, unless they looked carefully, that Holmes was a member of the court.

Holmes did not like this feature of judging on the highest court of a state. He thought that the practices of giving each judge an equal opportunity to write opinions for the court and of emphasizing unanimous decisions worked to de-emphasize the contributions of the more gifted judges, who could analyze legal issues more quickly and deeply than their colleagues. Throughout his career as a lawyer, legal scholar, and judge, Holmes had demonstrated two talents that set him apart from his peers: the ability to cut to the heart of a legal problem in a comparatively short time and the ability to absorb and to digest vast amounts of material. Those talents made him a remarkably fast worker, someone who could make up his mind on a case quickly and could develop impressive arguments to support his position. In addition, Holmes was a gifted writer, with an instinct for memorable phrases and an ability to express his thoughts in language that combined brevity and depth. In short, he was an ideal candidate to write judicial opinions. "I should like to decide every case," he wrote Clare Castletown in 1897, "and write every judgment of the court, but I'm afraid the boys [his colleagues] wouldn't see it."

A persistent theme of Holmes's relations with his fellow judges, whether on the Supreme Judicial Court of Massachusetts or later on the Supreme Court of the United States, was that he felt somewhat frustrated by the collegial decision-making process. On the Massachusetts court he had six judicial colleagues; on the Supreme Court he was one of nine justices. He had to take into account the views of his colleagues at every level of his job. They heard arguments along with him; they participated in the conferences in which, after a case had been argued, it was discussed and decided; they reacted to, criticized, and sometimes modified his views on legal questions; they were involved in the process by which opinions were assigned; they needed to approve of the opinions he produced and sometimes objected to his reasoning or his language. Holmes rarely quarreled openly with his fellow judges—in his 50 years of judging there was no colleague from which he became significantly estranged—but he regarded many of them as obstacles standing in the way of his efforts to "say his say on every question which the law has ever presented."

When Holmes described how he felt about being a judge on the Supreme Judicial Court of Massachusetts to others, he alternated between general expressions of satisfaction with the work of deciding cases and feelings of frustration. He was satisfied to be holding a job in which he constantly made important decisions and to have the skills that made that job easy. "I feel like Dr. Somebody," he wrote to a friend in 1901, "who said that pure surgery was the highest pleasure of which the human mind was capable." This comment was prompted by his belief that during a year in which he had been chief justice of his court, "we are smashing through the docket & everything is going with whiz [great speed]." But a few years earlier, in an 1897 letter to Clare Castletown, he said that he was "grinding my teeth in secret rage at the public ignorance of the difference between the first rate and the second rate," an ignorance "I apply to myself."

Holmes had fully expected, on choosing to immerse himself in the law in the early 1870s, to become as big a celebrity as his father. But when his father died in 1894, that was not the case: The father was a celebrated figure with a national reputation, the son an obscure Massachusetts judge. And when Holmes reached his 20th year on the Supreme Court of Massachusetts in 1902, he still was relatively obscure, still the son of a famous father. But then an opportunity for fame appeared, and Holmes seized it.

Holmes at age 61, in 1902, the year he was appointed to the U.S. Supreme Court. He continued to wear high-necked collars, and to cultivate the mustache he had grown during the Civil War, until his death in 1935.

5

A MORE IMPORTANT AND MORE VISIBLE COURT

In 1901, as Holmes turned 60 and anticipated his third year as chief justice of the Supreme Judicial Court of Massachusetts, a series of events began to unfold that resulted in his being appointed to the U.S. Supreme Court. During the previous year Justice Horace Gray of the Supreme Court, the half-brother of Holmes's friend John Gray, had developed an illness that made his retirement from the Court at the end of its term that June a possibility. For most of the years of the Supreme Court's existence, geography has played an important part in appointments. For the first two-thirds of the 19th century the Court met only briefly in Washington and for the rest of the year the justices traveled on "circuits" around the country—each circuit consisting of several states—and decided appeals from the federal district courts that were assigned to their circuit. There was a New England circuit, a circuit including New York State and Vermont, a circuit including Pennsylvania, Delaware, and Maryland, and so on. As the nation expanded westward, and new states came into the Union, new circuits were added: Now there are 11.

It was assumed that when a justice of the Court retired, died, or resigned, his successor would come from the same circuit. In most cases the successor would come from the same state as the departing justice, because one state usually provided most of the legal business of the circuit to which it was assigned. In the case of the First Circuit, or New England circuit, Massachusetts provided the dominant share of business. So when Horace Gray communicated his intention to retire to President William McKinley, McKinley assumed that the new justice would come from Massachusetts.

Because McKinley was not particularly familiar with Massachusetts legal or political circles, he consulted his secretary of the navy, who happened to be John Davis Long, the man who as governor of Massachusetts had nominated Holmes to the Supreme Judicial Court. But Long did not advise McKinley to nominate Holmes. Instead he recommended Alfred Hemenway, with whom he had been in law practice after his term as governor ended. McKinley asked Gray to announce his retirement shortly before the Supreme Court began its fall term in October 1901, at which point he would announce the appointment of Hemenway as Gray's successor.

Had McKinley's plans worked out, Holmes would almost certainly not have become a justice of the Supreme Court of the United States. In 1901 he was 60 years old, and no additional resident of Massachusetts would be appointed to the Court until Hemenway left it. Most justices appointed to the Court remain there for at least 10 years, and the chances were that by the time Hemenway left, Holmes would have been considered too old to be appointed.

But then on September 6, 1901, while greeting the public after making a speech in Buffalo, New York, President McKinley was shot by a deranged assassin and died on September 14. McKinley's Vice President,

Theodore Roosevelt, became President of the United States. Roosevelt did not feel obligated to nominate Hemenway, whom he did not know, and so Justice Gray did not announce his retirement but returned to the Court in October for another year.

In February Gray had a stroke, and it became obvious that he would need to retire. Roosevelt did not wait until Gray formally retired before beginning the process of naming his successor. Because the nominee was likely to come from Massachusetts, the attitudes of

A 1900 campaign poster for President William McKinley, who was reelected only to be assassinated a year later.

George Frisbee Hoar, who was still the senior senator from that state, and Henry Cabot Lodge, the junior senator, were important. This was both to Holmes's advantage and disadvantage. Hoar, who had opposed Holmes for the federal district judgeship in 1878, still had a negative opinion of him. Lodge, on the other hand, had been a close friend of Holmes since his childhood. Both were Harvard graduates and had been members of the same social club there, the Porcellian. Roosevelt, too, was a Harvard graduate and a member of Porcellian; he was also a close friend of Lodge's. By the spring of 1902, three months before Gray's formal retirement, Lodge had decided that Holmes was his first choice for the nomination.

After Gray's stroke, Holmes's close friends realized that his connections to Lodge and to Roosevelt made him a serious candidate for the Supreme Court seat. One of

Holmes's close female friends, Nina Gray, the wife of his old friend John Gray, wrote him, "Now that Horace has himself announced that he is not going back to Washington, I am in suspense wondering what is to happen. Will Mr. Hoar put his finger in the pie, or will you have what you want (or at least what you wish to have offered to you)?" She recognized that if Hoar had the opportunity to weigh in publicly on Holmes's nomination, he might succeed in blocking it.

Holmes remained Roosevelt's first choice as the summer of 1902 approached. But there was one piece of information about Holmes that gave Roosevelt pause. He was not sure how committed Holmes was to the Republican party. "In the higher sense, in the proper sense," Roosevelt wrote to Lodge, "a judge of the Supreme Court is not fitted for the position unless he is a party man." By a "party man" Roosevelt meant one "in entire sympathy with our views, that is your views and mine," and "absolutely sane and sound on the great national policies for which we stand in public life."

Roosevelt needed to know that Holmes shared his political views. Presidents who nominate Supreme Court justices regularly seek such reassurance, despite the fact that once a person joins the Supreme Court, he or she may consider a number of issues, over the years, that the nominating President never anticipated.

In his letter to Lodge, Roosevelt mentioned one legal question on which he particularly wanted to know Holmes's views. The question had been a major issue in the 1900 election: It involved the constitutional status of the colonial territories of the United States, such as Puerto Rico and the Philippines. In 1901 the Supreme Court heard a case that tested the constitutionality of tariffs on sugar and tobacco products produced in those territories. Because inhabitants of those territories were not permitted to vote in U.S. elections, they argued that for Congress to force them to pay tariffs on the sugar and tobacco they shipped into the United States amounted to taxation without representation. They also argued that Congress could not impose tariffs on goods shipped from one U.S. state to another. Finally, they argued that although Puerto Rico and the Philippines had not been granted statehood, they were U.S. territories, and thus their inhabitants were entitled to the same constitutional protections as U.S. citizens.

These arguments had all been made by the Democratic candidate for President, William Jennings Bryan, in the 1900 election. Leading Democratic politicians continued to endorse this position in the first decade of the 20th century. McKinley and other Republican politicians argued, however, that until Congress chose to incorporate U.S. territories into the Union, their residents remained outside the protection of the U.S. Constitution. Congress might choose to grant them the rights of U.S. citizens or treat the territories as the equivalent of states, but it had no obligation to do so.

In 1901 the Supreme Court, by a 5-to-4 majority, agreed with the position of the Republican party. Horace Gray had been a member of that majority, and Roosevelt, who felt very strongly about the sovereign powers of the United States in its dealings with overseas possessions, wanted to be sure that any person he nominated to the Court would continue to support the majority position.

Lodge was not worried about Holmes's position on the constitutional status of overseas territories. He knew that Holmes believed that nations, including the United States, had nearly unlimited power to conduct their international affairs as they chose—unless, in the case of the United States, a particular power had been expressly taken away by the Constitution. The only restriction on the exercise of

A 1922 photograph of Holmes's close friend Nina Lyman Gray, the wife of John Chipman Gray, Holmes's fellow Civil War survivor, Harvard Law School colleague, and friend. Nina Gray was one of Holmes's most frequent correspondents: From the 1880s until her death in 1933 he wrote her about his ambitions, his flirtations, and his judicial work.

foreign relations powers specifically mentioned in the Constitution was that the President, who had the power to make treaties with foreign nations, needed the consent of two-thirds of the Senate before a treaty was official. There was no language in the Constitution restricting the President or Congress in their dealings with overseas territories. Congress could also incorporate federal territories into the Union at its pleasure. So Lodge was confident that Holmes would be a strong supporter of the Republican position, which, after he joined the Court, he was.

To be on the safe side, however, Lodge assured Roosevelt that he would put the concerns about the proper treatment of overseas territories "to Holmes with absolute frankness." In addition, a secret meeting was arranged between Roosevelt and Holmes at Roosevelt's summer home, Sagamore Hill, in Oyster Bay, New York, to take place on July 25, 1902. At the meeting Roosevelt intended to sound out Holmes about his views on the constitutional status of overseas territories. After the meeting Holmes wrote Nina Gray that Roosevelt "said just the right things and impressed me far more than I had expected." He noted in his journal that on July 25 the "Presdt. offered me Judgeship."

Senator Henry Cabot Lodge, the junior Senator from Massachusetts at the time Roosevelt named Holmes to the Supreme Court. Lodge had known Holmes since his youth and was also a close friend of Roosevelt's. He was primarily responsible for securing Holmes the Supreme Court nomination.

Holmes accepted the offer. But Roosevelt did not release that information to the press or to the general public. His reason for delaying the announcement was to let Senator Hoar, whom Roosevelt and Lodge had deliberately bypassed in the nominating process, learn the news that Holmes was the choice. Both Roosevelt and Lodge expected that Hoar would not receive the news well, especially because his nephew had been mentioned as a candidate. But they also knew that Hoar was unlikely to make his reaction to the nomination public; his constituents might suppose that

Hoar's opposition was based on family loyalty or self-interest. Roosevelt and Lodge chose to inform Hoar at a time when they suspected he could do the least amount of damage to Holmes's candidacy.

Holmes was given a recess appointment, because the U.S. Senate, which confirms Supreme Court nominations, was not in session during the summer. He continued to work as chief justice of the Supreme Judicial Court and did not resign from that court, in fact, until he actually heard the news of his confirmation in early December 1902. In the meantime Senator Hoar attempted to stir up some opposition, although not publicly. He complained in a letter to Roosevelt that "the old method" of making Supreme Court nominations had not been followed in Holmes's case. The old method, as Hoar described it, was "to let the public know of the vacancy, to allow a reasonable time for all persons interested, especially the members of the legal profession and the representatives of the States immediately concerned, to make known their opinions and desires."

In November, before the Senate had acted on the nomination, Hoar made one last effort to undermine Holmes's nomination and wrote a letter to Melville Fuller, the chief justice of the United States. Hoar could not resist passing on what he believed to be a general opinion of Holmes among some members of the Massachusetts legal community. "The best lawyers of Massachusetts, almost without exception," Hoar informed Fuller,

> believe that while [Holmes] has excellent qualities, he is lacking in intellectual strength, and that his opinions carry with them no authority merely because they are his. We have contributed from New England some very tough oak timbers to the Bench, State and National. Our lawyers in general, especially those in the country, do not think that carved ivory is likely to be as strong or enduring, although it may seem more ornamental.

Given Holmes's scholarship in jurisprudence and legal history, the searching quality of many of his Massachusetts judicial opinions, and his reputation for knowing as much or more law than anyone in the Boston area, it is hard to understand, at first, what Hoar could have meant. A clue to his attitude, however, can be found in comments made by two newspapers on August 12, 1902, the day after Holmes's nomination had been formally announced. The *New York Evening Post* described Holmes as "more brilliant than sound" as a judge. And the *Boston Evening Transcript,* after characterizing Holmes as "more of a 'literary feller' than one often finds on the bench," said that Holmes's "striking originality will help ... when it does not hinder." Some observers of Holmes had concluded that in writing opinions, he tended to be more interested in going through an intricate legal analysis or in constructing memorable "literary" sentences than in making "sound" decisions that laid down sensible legal rules in a clear and predictable fashion.

This was a fair criticism of Holmes's approach to writing judicial opinions, but his tendencies cannot be associated with lack of "intellectual strength." On the contrary, Holmes liked to "see a case to the bottom," that is, to see its larger legal and intellectual significance. He liked to write opinions that demonstrated that his thought process had gone beyond the question of which party in the case should prevail, or even which legal rules should govern the case, to include a consideration of the social policies, or the legal philosophy, behind those rules. He also liked to write opinions that included memorable and original language. He acted, as few of his fellow judges did, as much as a philosopher and literary craftsman as a judge in the writing of opinions. As a result, he sometimes wrote obscurely, which sometimes made the practical meaning of his opinions—especially as guidelines for future cases—hard to determine.

Holmes was very much aware of this reaction to him as a judge. In a remarkable letter to his English friend

Frederick Pollock, written before the Senate had confirmed him, Holmes expressed his frustration at this negative reaction. "There have been tacks of notices of me all over the country," he told Pollock, and "they are so favorable that they make my nomination a popular success."

> [But] the immense majority of them seem to me hopelessly devoid of personal discrimination or courage.... They have the flabbiness of American ignorance.... As to my judicial career ... it is easy to suggest that the Judge has partial views, is brilliant but not very sound, has talent but is not great, etc. It makes one sick when he has broken his heart in trying to make every word living and real to see a lot of duffers, generally I think not even lawyers, talking with the sanctity of print in a way that at once discloses ... that literally they don't know anything about it.... You can understand how in a moment of ostensible triumph I have been in a desert—when I hoped to see that they understood what I meant.... If I haven't done my share in the way of putting in new and remodeling old thought for the last 20 years then I delude myself ... [and] in the main damn the lot of them.

The overwhelming majority of newspaper reactions to Holmes's nomination, as he mentioned, were favorable, however. An essayist in *The American Law Review* predicted that his career on the Supreme Court "will be no less brilliant than it has been in every work in which he has been engaged and in every position he has been called upon to fill." Holmes left Boston for Washington and the Supreme Court with a feeling of joy that he would still be making decisions, still be feeling his "power of work," and at the same time engaging in a new professional adventure on a more important and more visible Court. But, as he wrote to a friend, he was "very blue" in the midst of his triumph. He saw himself as still "half obscure" and misunderstood.

The Supreme Court of the United States in 1904. Every October, when the Court begins a new term, the justices assemble for a picture, seated in order of seniority with the chief justice in the middle of the front row. Holmes is at the far left of the back row. At the time of the photograph he was beginning his third year on the Court and was the second most junior justice.

A New and Solemn Volume Opens

Shortly after arriving in Washington, Holmes wrote to Frederick Pollock that his professional and personal life in Boston seemed like "a finished book—locked up far away, and a new and solemn volume opens." In other letters to friends written soon after beginning his work in December 1902, he spoke of the "mighty panorama of cases from every part of our great empire," the quality of the lawyers who argued cases before the Court ("the strongest men in the country"), the appearance of legal questions "I had never heard of," and the presence of "some very powerful men" among his new colleagues on the Court. The Supreme Court of the United States, he concluded, was "a center of great forces," and the justices interpreted the law "as statesmen governing an empire."

This was Holmes's initial reaction to becoming a Supreme Court justice, and there were other changes that suggested that he had indeed entered a new stage of his life. The most obvious change was moving from Boston to Washington. Holmes and Fanny had never lived anywhere except the Boston area. They had never owned their own home, moving from an apartment to Holmes Sr.'s house after the death of Holmes's sister Amelia in 1889, and remaining in the house after the death of Holmes Sr. at 85 in 1894. By the 1880s they had settled into a pattern: Holmes spent his days on his judicial work, walking from Beacon Street to the courthouse in downtown Boston and traveling, most summers, around the state to hear trial cases. Other summers, when he was not required to act as trial judge, he traveled to England. Fanny stayed in the Beacon Street house, first helping take care of Holmes Sr., then remaining largely by herself, occupied by her needlework embroideries, her birds, and her duties as household manager, which included paying the bills. In the evenings, if Holmes was not at a social gathering, Fanny often read aloud to him.

Boston was changing in the late 19th century, becoming a less important commercial city but remaining the most important center of American literary and cultural affairs. It also was a source of urban political reform and of increased tensions between old-stock "Yankees," such as the Holmeses, and Irish immigrants who had begun to involve themselves with city politics. But none of this touched Wendell and Fanny very much: They continued their domestic routines, which included summer vacations at Beverly Farms, near the coast north of Boston, where they had bought a house. The only major contrast to the Holmeses' life in Boston, for Wendell, was his summer visits to England, where he temporarily abandoned his focus on the law for literary and philosophical conversation and the company of Clare Castletown and other women that he found stimulating. In England, he wrote Nina Gray, he would rather talk to a pretty girl than a dull judge. When Holmes was confirmed as an Associate Justice of the Supreme Court of the United States, it became necessary for the Holmeses to move from Boston to Washington. They bought a house for the first time in their lives, on 1720 Eye Street in the Northwest of the city. Holmes wrote of the joy of owning his own house for the first time, and of the liberating feeling of cleaning out old papers and household effects from his father's Boston house. Fanny took the occasion to destroy most of her embroideries. Moving to Washington in 1902 meant hotter summers, the formalities of Southern society, the disappearance of the seacoast, and exposure to the world of national politics. The Holmeses took the train down along with their baggage and furniture. They decided to keep the Beverly Farms house so as to return to the Boston area in the summers.

Another major change involved Holmes's flirtations with women. When Holmes arrived in Washington, he found that the social conventions, at least for visible public officials, differed from those in Boston. In that city, he had been able to make regular calls on female friends and to develop relationships, such as that with Nina Gray, in which he could talk about his personal feelings and engage in light, flirtatious banter. Neither he nor Fanny seemed to regard his activities as a comment on their marriage, although it is not clear how much Fanny knew about Wendell's relationship with Clare Castletown.

The atmosphere in Washington was different from life in New England. Holmes believed, at least initially, that the demands of his new job would leave him no time for flirtations. In addition, his new position carried some social responsibilities with it: The wives of Supreme Court justices, like those of cabinet officials, were expected to hold weekly tea parties and entertain members of Washington political society. The Holmeses were also regularly invited to official dinners, some at the White House. Fanny, who had become more reclusive in Boston as the years went on, was suddenly thrust into a position of having to entertain and attend parties. Holmes was delighted to find that she was a success as a hostess and rather enjoyed herself as a guest. "I don't in the slightest degree wish to find an egeria [a woman companion] here," he told his old Boston friend,

The White House dining room near the turn of the century. The Holmeses often attended White House dinners in the early 1900s, but after Holmes's dissent in the Northern Securities *case in November 1904, Theodore Roosevelt stopped inviting them.*

Ellen Curtis. "As my wife goes with me everywhere I have all the companionship I need."

In addition to Fanny's new role and the increased interest in his job, Holmes discovered another feature of Washington life that may have had an effect on him. That was the relatively formal arrangement of companions at social gatherings, dictated in large part by the importance of one's professional position. As a justice of the Supreme Court, Holmes was an important figure, not likely to be paired off at a party with the kind of attractive young woman whose company he tended to seek out. "I dine out a good deal," he wrote to Ellen Curtis, "often being assigned a lady on principle of precedence not of selection." The ones he might have selected for companionship, he added, "I meet only for a flitting moment." Moreover, in a city filled with gossip about public officials, he felt "that eternal discretion is necessary." "It is strange," he told Nina Gray, "how small a part the society of women plays in my life here. Apart from memory I hardly should know that they existed."

Holmes, however, kept up his friendships with Nina Gray, Clare Castletown, and several other women, and his correspondence during his years as a Supreme Court justice included nearly as many letters to women as to men. But the tone and topics did not vary a great deal whether he was writing to a man or a woman. He wrote mainly about the books he was reading and the ideas that interested him, not very much about his work on the Court and very little about relationships.

In fact, Holmes's absorption with his new job, and his belief that it might take up all his time and energy, was relatively short-lived. Within a year of becoming a Supreme Court justice, he had learned once again that, as he put it, he could grasp in a minute legal issues that it took some of his colleagues a quarter of an hour to unravel. In addition, he had learned that he could produce opinions as rapidly as he had as a Massachusetts judge. Holmes encountered many new kinds of cases on the Supreme Court, but the process of deciding them and writing opinions remained the same.

The basement courtroom in the old Senate chamber at the Capitol, where the Supreme Court met during Holmes's tenure.

After 20 years on the Supreme Judicial Court of Massachusetts, he had a lot of experience.

When Holmes joined the Court in 1902, it used a procedure for assigning opinions similar to that employed by the Supreme Judicial Court of Massachusetts. After the Court had heard the lawyers for both sides argue the disputed questions of law in a case, the justices met in conference to decide those questions. During Holmes's time on the Supreme Court, the conference meetings took place in a room in the basement of the Capitol in Washington, near to where the Supreme Court courtroom itself was located. The Court did not have its own building at the time (one was built in the mid-1930s, after Holmes had retired). The justices worked at their homes in Washington and traveled to the Court for arguments and conferences. Holmes often made the 25-minute walk to the Capitol from his house at 1720 Eye Street.

Arguments before the Supreme Court started about noon and could last three or four hours. The justices heard cases on most of the days that the Court was in session but did not hold conferences more than once a week. Conferences themselves could last three hours. No one was permitted in the Supreme Court's conference room except the judges themselves. No formal notes were taken of the conferences, although some individual justices took notes. The entire proceedings were confidential, and justices were not supposed to discuss what had happened within the conference room with anyone else.

The chief justice was responsible for setting the agenda of a particular conference, introducing the cases to be discussed, and stating his views on each. His remarks were followed by each of the other justices in order of seniority, with the associate justice who had been on the Court longest speaking next. A second round of discussions then took place in which each judge stated his vote on the legal questions at issue. When the chief justice knew what all the votes were in a case, he assigned the responsibility of writing the opinion to a member of the majority, who might be himself. If he had not voted with the majority, the power to assign an opinion was transferred to the senior associate justice who was with the majority. In Holmes's day most of the decisions made by the Supreme Court were unanimous, and the assignment power normally went to the chief justice. In general, opinions were equally assigned among the justices.

Some justices enjoyed writing opinions more than others, and some were able to produce opinions more quickly than others. Holmes both enjoyed writing opinions and could produce them rapidly. He told Chief Justice Melville Fuller shortly after joining the Court that he could typically produce an opinion in two days. The Court's conference day during Fuller's tenure was Saturday, and Holmes would be assigned an opinion on most Saturdays. He would complete it by the following Wednesday and ask for another assignment, which, if he received, he would complete by the Saturday conference. Most of the other judges never came close to working that fast.

Although Fuller appreciated Holmes's quick work, it also had the potential to cause problems. Holmes was eager to be assigned more opinions, and if Fuller had granted every request for an additional opinion, Holmes would soon have been writing most of the Court's opinions, and other justices might have resented that. So Fuller actually made efforts to slow down the progress of Holmes's work.

Holmes's writing style also had an effect on his fellow justices. By the time Holmes joined the Supreme Court, the judges had developed a habit of circulating their opinions to the other judges who had voted the same way during conference before formally issuing the opinion. This had not always been the Court's practice, but over time some justices had objected to the reasoning behind decisions they supported and had even written "concurring" opinions, in which they agreed with the majority result but for different reasons.

Holmes, too, made a practice of circulating his majority opinions before they were formally issued. Fellow justices sometimes objected to Holmes's language and sometimes complained that his opinions were too brief, with the result that his reasoning was not completely understandable. Holmes did not, on the whole, appreciate those objections from his colleagues. He felt they were excessively cautious about language, particularly language in which he tried to be creative or original, and they were sometimes slow to follow reasoning that he believed was appropriately brief and to the point. "I don't believe in the long opinions which have been almost the rule here," he wrote Nina Gray soon after joining the Court. He preferred "to state the case shortly and the ground of decision as concisely and delicately as you can."

Holmes was not particularly interested in finding a common ground with other judges who shared his views on a case; once given the assignment of writing an opinion, he wanted to put his distinctive stamp on it. Because he penetrated quickly to the fundamental questions of law and policy at stake, he did not feel inclined to labor over the steps of his thought process and explain it to others; he would rather write his opinions, as he put it, "with style," using memorable language to give his readers something to think about. He was less interested in spelling out in detail the guidelines for those interested in the case as a set of rules for the conduct of affairs. One of Holmes's great admirers, Harvard law professor and future Supreme Court justice Felix Frankfurter, said that in most instances Holmes "spoke for the

Louis Dembitz Brandeis in 1916, the year of his appointment to the Supreme Court. Brandeis, who served on the Court until 1939, was Holmes's closest friend on it and, in the view of Chief Justice William Howard Taft, a decisive influence on Holmes's positions in cases during the later years of his career.

Court tersely and often cryptically." John Gray once suggested that Holmes's opinions "seemed to lack lucidity."

Holmes, however, maintained cordial relations with most of his judicial colleagues, although he had few close friends among his fellow justices. And in general he was not concerned with the internal politics of the Court, although he did seek out, and apparently enjoyed the company of, Chief Justices Fuller and Edward White, because those men had the power to assign him cases. He reserved close friendship for those justices whom he considered his intellectual equals, most conspicuously Louis Brandeis.

Brandeis, a native of Louisville, Kentucky, graduated from Harvard Law School in 1877 at the age of 20, having achieved the highest grade average in the history of that school up to that point. He went on to have a successful career as a lawyer in Boston and as an adviser to President Woodrow Wilson, who nominated him to the Supreme Court in 1916. Brandeis was the first Jewish justice to sit on the Court, and his nomination was controversial, in part because of the anti-Semitic attitudes of some of his opponents. Brandeis had first met Holmes as a young lawyer in Boston, and the two justices had a mutual respect for each other. Brandeis was extremely interested in the political implications of cases, tending to take a progressive, or liberal, philosophical stance.

Brandeis also had his own views on how opinions should be written. He believed in relatively lengthy, detailed opinions, with the legal arguments extensively supported by references to previous cases or to social and economic data. At the beginning of his career his opinions looked somewhat like the written arguments, called briefs, that lawyers file with a court as part of their presentation. On one occasion Holmes read a draft opinion Brandeis had written and wrote a note that said, "I can't think it good form to put in footnotes." Brandeis, for his part, thought that Holmes's opinions were too short, sometimes lacking supporting evidence, and filled with colorful phrases whose meanings were often obscure or ambiguous. Brandeis also felt that Holmes sometimes seemed more interested in getting his opinions written than in making them understandable.

Holmes had a tendency, as Brandeis once put it, to "fire off" when assigned an opinion to write. Once Holmes had thought through a legal problem, he tended to find that it recurred in only slightly different forms in subsequent cases. He did not want to write at any length, or even to express any disagreements with the majority in the form of a dissenting opinion, if he had earlier expressed his thoughts. Brandeis, on the other hand, felt that persistent dissents on important legal issues were necessary in order to put pressure on a majority to change its views. He thus encouraged Holmes to write dissents in many cases in which Holmes felt that he had already gone through the exercise of "saying his say" on the legal questions and was inclined to simply record his vote in opposition.

Brandeis once said that Holmes had "no realization of what moves men—he is as innocent as a girl of sixteen." Holmes "ought to have more influence with the Court," Brandeis felt, but his tendency to "fire off" on the abstract intellectual dimensions of a case often made him blind to the political motivations of some of his colleagues. And his tendency to try to find a "form of words" that was unique and original made his opinions attractive to read but hard to decipher. "Holmes did not sufficiently consider the need of others to understand," Brandeis once said of his friend.

An illustration of the way Holmes approached the job of deciding cases came in an important antitrust case: *Northern Securities Co.* v. *United States.* The Court decided the case in 1904, the second year Holmes sat on it. When Roosevelt had appointed Holmes to the Court, he had written to Senator Lodge that Holmes was "our kind—right through." By that he meant not only that Holmes shared his social and intellectual instincts but that he was sympathetic

This antitrust cartoon depicting Standard Oil as an octopus appeared in Puck *magazine in September 1904, the year the* Northern Securities *case was decided.*

to the "progressive" wing of the Republican party, of which Roosevelt was the symbolic leader.

The Progressives—who eventually became a third national party, with Theodore Roosevelt as their presidential candidate in the 1912 election—represented a diverse group of people united in their conviction that traditional U.S. government had not been responsive enough to some of the problems associated with the growth of a large urban and industrial society. Progressives believed that industrial workers should have better working conditions and higher wages. They thought the large corporations that dominated certain markets, such as railroads, iron and steel companies, and sugar manufacturers, should be prevented by government legislation from becoming too large or having too big a share of their markets. Progressives had a number of other goals as well, ranging from beautifying cities to stomping out corruption in municipal government to reducing the number of immigrants allowed to enter the United States. They called themselves Progressives because they believed that humans could make the future better than the past and that reforming the government and society would amount to progress.

When the *Northern Securities* case was argued before the Supreme Court, Roosevelt and his Republican party were identified with reform.

The most visible and controversial reform effort was the Roosevelt administration's attempt to dissolve some of the large trust companies. A trust company was the popular name for a holding company, which is a corporation whose sole purpose is to hold the stock of more than one company in the same business. Holding companies, or trusts, were formed when business competitors merged in order to dominate a market, reduce competition, and control the prices charged for products.

In 1890 Congress had passed legislation, known as the Sherman Anti-Trust Act, that outlawed "combinations in the form of trusts" or "conspiracies" that "restrained trade" when the combining businesses operated in interstate commerce. If the language of the legislation were taken literally, it meant that no businesses, however small, could enter into agreements with their competitors if their products crossed state lines. The language of the Sherman Anti-Trust Act was so broad that the government did not attempt to enforce it for several years, but after Roosevelt became President, his administration decided to try to enforce it by bringing an antitrust suit against the Northern Securities Company, a holding company that had been created by two competing railroads operating in a region where a third railroad operated as well. Roosevelt's attorney general argued, in a case that eventually went to the Supreme Court, that the creation of holding companies by competitors in the railroad business was outlawed by the Sherman Act.

In a 5-to-4 decision, the Supreme Court agreed. Holmes, however, dissented. He thought that if one read the plain words Congress had written in the Sherman Anti-Trust Act, only two interpretations were possible. Either Congress meant to outlaw every combination or every contract made between two entities that participated in interstate commerce, or it simply meant to outlaw the kinds of contracts that had regularly been found to be illegal in previous common law decisions by courts, such as those made by monopolies to keep other companies from coming into their markets. Holmes felt that it was absurd to think that Congress meant to make "every combination, the small as well as the great," illegal. So the act, Holmes reasoned, must be limited to those contracts or combinations that were regarded as harmful before its passage. The Northern Securities Company, although it had been established to give two railroad companies a competitive advantage, was not a monopoly: It did not seek to end all other interstate railroad business in its particular region. So the Sherman Anti-Trust Act, Holmes concluded, did not apply, and the Northern Securities Company should not be dissolved.

When the *Northern Securities* decision was announced by the Court, Roosevelt, although gratified with the result, was furious that the first justice he had appointed had conspicuously rejected an interpretation of the antitrust laws to which the Roosevelt administration was committed. Two years later Roosevelt had still not forgotten. He wrote to Henry Cabot Lodge:

> Nothing has been so strongly borne in on me concerning lawyers on the bench as that the *nominal* politics of the man has nothing to do with his actions on the bench. His *real* politics are all important. From his antecedents, Holmes should have been an ideal man for the bench. As a matter of fact he has been a bitter disappointment.

Roosevelt had misunderstood Holmes's "real politics" as a judge. Holmes was not interested in the short-run political consequences of Supreme Court decisions. He was interested in the larger questions of economic policy, such as whether government regulation had any significant effect on the distribution of wealth or on the effectiveness of markets for goods and services (he did not believe it did). He felt strongly that his positions should be consistent with the appropriate role for judges in a constitutional democracy, whether or not those positions led to results that he might favor as an individual. In the *Northern Securities* case he had been asked to decide whether the Sherman Act applied to a particular economic arrangement, and he concluded that it would be straining the meaning of the act to apply it to that arrangement. This did not mean that he liked or disliked either the statute or the existence of trusts such as the Northern Securities Company. He had simply decided a question of law on intellectual grounds.

Holmes's position in the *Northern Securities* case was illustrative of his stance during his entire career on the Supreme Court of the United States. Although he wrote a number of opinions in cases that were perceived as having major short-run political significance, he did not consider the immediate political consequences of a case in making his decision. In fact, he thought those consequences often were a distraction and even a barrier to effective judicial analysis. "Great cases … make bad law," he wrote in his *Northern Securities* dissent. "For great cases are called great, not by reason of their real importance in shaping the law of the future, but because of some accident of immediate over-whelming interest which appeals to the feelings and distorts the judgment."

Holmes was strikingly detached from politics: He never read a newspaper during his tenure on the Court; as a resident of the District of Columbia, he could not vote in presidential elections; and his correspondence did not contain references to national political issues or debates. For him, judging was primarily an exercise in legal theory, and in many cases he thought that his appropriate theoretical posture was to defer to legislatures, because they were more representative of popular views in a democracy. Holmes was definitely not a "party man" as a judge, not even in the "high sense" in which Roosevelt described it. And his "real politics" did not include thinking about whether his decisions pleased the President who had appointed him.

AN UNEXPECTED DISSENT

In Northern Securities Co. v. United States (1904) the Supreme Court favored the viewpoint of Theodore Roosevelt's administration and broke up the Northern Securities Co. by enforcing the Sherman Anti-Trust Act of 1890. In his dissent Holmes said that he believed the company was not the type of trust prohibited by the Act. On hearing of Holmes's dissent, Roosevelt reportedly said that a judge with more backbone could have been carved out of a banana.

Great cases like hard cases make bad law. For great cases are called great, not by reason of their real importance in shaping the law of the future, but because of some accident of immediate overwhelming interest which appeals to the feelings and distorts the judgment. These immediate interests exercise a kind of hydraulic pressure which makes what previously was clear seem doubtful, and before which even well settled principles of law will bend. What we have to do in this case is to find the meaning of some not very difficult words.... [W]hile at times judges need for their work the training of economists or statesmen ... yet when their task is to interpret and apply the words of a statute, their function is ... to read English intelligently, and a consideration of consequences comes into play, if at all, only when the meaning of words is open to reasonable doubt....

The law ... says nothing about competition, and only prevents its suppression by contracts or combinations in restraint of trade, and such contracts or combinations derive their character as restraining trade from other features than the suppression of competition alone.... If I am ... wrong [in my interpretation of the Sherman Anti-Trust Law], then a partnership between two stage drivers who had been competitors in driving across a state line ... if now continued, is a crime. For ... if the restraint on the freedom of the members of a combination caused by their entering into partnership is a restraint of trade, every such combination, as well the small as the great, is within the act.

AN UNLIKELY
REFORMER

As Holmes entered his second decade on the Supreme
Court, he began to take judicial positions that made him
appear to be a critic of the established economic order.
Progressive legislatures had begun to try to regulate the
working hours and wages of industrial laborers, hoping to
guarantee an eight-hour day or a minimum wage, and
those laws were now being challenged on constitutional
grounds. The challenges were based on the idea that both
employers and employees had a constitutional right to buy
and sell their services on the terms they chose—the "liberty
of contract," as it was called. It was thought to be an interference with this liberty for legislatures to impose maxi-
mum-hour or minimum-wage restrictions on businesses, or
to prohibit contracts that made a worker's employment
conditional on his promise not to join a union. In a series
of cases from 1905 through the 1920s—*Lochner* v. *New
York, Adair* v. *United States, Coppage* v. *Kansas,* and *Adkins* v.
Children's Hospital—a majority of the Supreme Court
struck down this progressive legislation.

The Court based its decisions on an interpretation of
the due process clauses of the 5th and 14th Amendments to

Wreckage of the Triangle Shirtwaist Company's factory, where 146 female workers lost their lives in a fire in 1911. Inadequate ventilation and the absence of fire exits contributed to the loss of life; the exposure of such conditions, which were typical of many American businesses in the early 20th century, contributed to demands for legislation to improve the working lives of industrial laborers.

the U.S. Constitution. Both amendments state that a person shall not be deprived of "life, liberty, or property, without due process of law." No more detailed definition of "liberty" or "due process of law" is supplied in the constitutional text, however.

Until the middle of the 19th century, comparatively few cases asked courts to interpret the meaning of these phrases. But occasionally in the 1850s, and more commonly from the 1880s on, lawyers for property owners and industrial enterprises began to mount constitutional challenges to federal and state regulation. The overwhelming number of these challenges involved state efforts to regulate businesses. By the close of the century, a majority of the Court had expressed sympathy with those challenges, believing, for example, that when a state legislature attempted to prevent out-of-state insurance companies from insuring property within the state, that was an interference with the "liberty" of those companies to enter into business relations.

"Liberty of contract" in such cases seemed to be straightforward enough: In the insurance case, it meant the freedom of the company to enter into contracts with citizens of a different state. But as the 20th century opened, the term "liberty of contract" began to mean a "liberty" on the part of both parties to enter into the terms of that contract.

Very few labor unions existed in the first two decades of the 20th century, and many industrial workers did not have the education or specialized skills that would give them a wide variety of job prospects. When they applied for jobs at factories or industrial plants, they could accept the job on the terms proposed by the employer or look elsewhere for work. Progressive social theorists believed that the lack of bargaining power on the part of workers made it senseless to think of them as having any real "liberty" to hire themselves out on the terms they chose. In fact, many employers tended to take advantage of the poor bargaining position of prospective employees, with the result that a large percentage of the early-20th-century industrial work force labored under substandard conditions and endured excessively long work hours and shockingly low wages. Theorists also felt that the unionization of industrial workers would provide a mechanism for improving their bargaining power; wages would rise, work hours would be less demanding, and working conditions would improve.

Because progressive thinkers had no confidence that employers would voluntarily improve the wages or working conditions of their employees, they concluded that state and federal legislation imposing minimum wages and maximum work hours was the only solution. Similarly, because they thought that employers had no incentives to recognize labor unions but did have reasons to try to keep their employees from joining unions, reformers concluded that states had to pass laws that prohibited employers from insisting that those they hired sign contracts in which they agreed never to join a union. Such contracts were called "yellow dog" contracts because union sympathizers called workers who signed them "yellow dogs," or cowards.

Minimum wages, maximum hours, and anti-"yellow dog" legislation were extremely controversial in the early 20th century. Labor unrest had surfaced in the late 19th century, and strikes, boycotts, court injunctions against labor picketers, and occasional violence had become a feature of industrial life. Against this backdrop, a number of states and the federal government attempted to pass minimum-wage laws and laws preventing the use of "yellow dog" contracts. Such laws were immediately challenged by various employers on the ground that they amounted to a denial of both the employer's and the employee's liberty to enter into contracts on the terms they chose. By imposing minimum wages and maximum hours when employees would have been willing to be paid less and work longer, the legislation simply took money from an employer and gave it to the employee without any "due process." Those

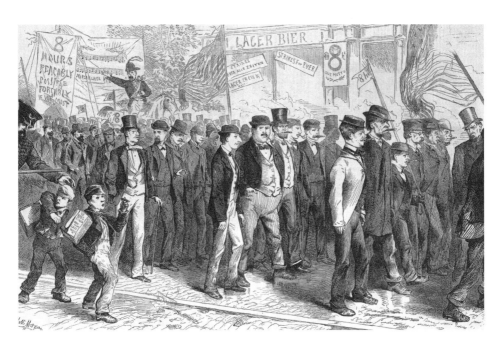

The U.S. labor movement had become established after the end of the Civil War, as illustrated by this 1872 cartoon showing strikers petitioning for an eight-hour workday. During Holmes's career on the Supreme Court, however, legislation requiring employers to limit the hours of their employees was consistently held unconstitutional by a majority. Sometimes Holmes wrote opinions in dissent.

who challenged these laws suggested that there was no reasonable basis, such as public health or safety, for the legislation. The laws, they said, were arbitrary efforts on the part of the legislature to substitute their view of the appropriate conditions of industrial employment for the conditions that were created by freedom of contract in the marketplace.

A majority of the Supreme Court, for the duration of Holmes's tenure, agreed with these arguments. Occasionally, the Court concluded that a public health rationale—such as protecting physically vulnerable women or workers in dangerous industries, such as mining—allowed a state to limit working hours, but in general the Court refused to permit states or the federal government to interfere with the terms of employment, advancing the "liberty of contract" implied in the due process clauses of the 5th and 14th Amendments as its justification.

The four decisions previously mentioned were particularly representative of this attitude on the part of the Court majority. In *Lochner* v. *New York* (1905) the owner of a bakery successfully challenged an effort on the part of the New

"THEY DO NOT CREATE SOMETHING OUT OF NOTHING"

Holmes had gained a reputation on the Supreme Judicial Court of Mass-achusetts as a radical on labor issues, because he endorsed the rights of workers to strike and to boycott companies whose labor practices they felt were unfair. In this passage Holmes explains his view that although industrial laborers might improve their financial position through strikes and boycotts, the cost of increased wages would be passed back to them, as they were also consumers of the goods they produced. Thus to endorse strikes was not necessarily to side with "labor" against "capital." The following passage is an example of how Holmes's opinions on political issues of his day had a tendency to be misunderstood.

Although this is not the place for extended economic discussion, and although the law may not always reach ultimate economic conceptions, I think it well to add that I cherish no illusions as to the meaning and effect of strikes. I think it pure phantasy to suppose that there is a body of capital of which labor as a whole secures a larger share by that means. The annual product, subject to an infinitesimal deduction for the luxuries of the few, is directed to consumption by the multitude, and is consumed by the multitude, always. Organization and strikes may get a larger share for the members of an organization, but, if they do, they get it at the expense of the less organized and less powerful portion of the laboring mass. They do not create something out of nothing.... But, subject to the qualifications which I have expressed, I think it lawful for a body of workmen to try by combination to get more than they now are getting, although they do it at the expense of their fellow, and to that end to strengthen their union by the boycott and the strike.

York state legislature to limit the workweek of bakers to 60 hours. In *Adair* v. *United States* (1908) the Court invalidated the Erdman Act of 1898, in which Congress prohibited "yellow dog" contracts in the interstate railroad industry. A manager of a railroad fired one of his employees for belonging to a union and was fined for violating the act. He successfully argued that the "liberty of contract" doctrine allowed the railroad to insist on no union membership as a condition of employment. In *Coppage* v. *Kansas* (1915) a similar law passed by the Kansas legislature was struck down.

In 1917 a decision upholding work-hour limitations imposed by the state of Oregon suggested that the Court might be backing away from a broad interpretation of "liberty of contract." But in *Adkins* v. *Children's Hospital* (1923) the Court struck down a law that imposed minimum wages for women and children employed in the District of Columbia. The legislation, which was pending in several states at the same time, was based on the principle of protecting women and children from the health problems associated with excessively long work hours by guaranteeing them enough money to work a shorter day. It was challenged by a female hospital worker who had lost her job because her employer, the Children's Hospital of the District of Columbia, did not want to continue to employ her at the higher rates imposed by the minimum-wage law. The Court majority—noting the passage of the 19th Amendment, giving women the right to vote, in 1920— declared that women now held full citizenship privileges and could not be given legal protection simply because of their sex.

Holmes dissented in all of these cases, in which the Court majority rested its decision on the "liberty of contract" doctrine. He argued that the concept of a constitutional "liberty of contract" was a fiction. He did not find it in the text of the Constitution, nor did he believe it was an inviolate principle of economic relations. Because legislatures represented the majority of citizens, they could regulate economic affairs unless the Constitution expressly forbid them from doing so. When judges created doctrines such as "liberty of contract," they were substituting their views on issues of political economy for those of the majority. They were not authorized to do that unless the Constitution mandated it. Holmes conveyed these views, in striking language, for the duration of his career on the Supreme Court. In his dissent in *Lochner v. New York* he said that "a constitution is not intended to embody a particular economic theory" and that the word "liberty in the Fourteenth Amendment is perverted when it is held to prevent the natural outcome of a dominant opinion."

Lochner's Bakery, 250 South Street, Utica, New York. This picture shows Joseph Lochner, the owner, second from the right, and the large amount of flour dust, which some of the justices who decided Lochner v. New York *thought to be unhealthy to bakery workers.*

THE CASE FOR MAJORITY RULE

In Holmes's dissent in Lochner v. New York *(1905), he argued that the Supreme Court should not overturn laws passed by legislatures simply because the justices want to promote a different policy. Instead, he wrote, the Court should limit itself to deciding whether such laws are constitutional.*

This case is decided upon an economic theory which a large part of the country does not entertain. If it were a question whether I agreed with that theory, I should desire to study it further and long before making up my mind. But I do not conceive that to be my duty, because I strongly believe that my agreement or disagreement has nothing to do with the right of a majority to embody their opinions in law.... The other day we sustained the Massachusetts vaccination law. United States and state statutes and decisions cutting down the liberty of contract ... are familiar to this Court.... The decision sustaining an eight-hour law for miners is still recent.

Some of these laws embody convictions or prejudices which judges are not likely to share. Some may not. But a constitution is not intended to embody a particular economic theory, whether of paternalism ... or of laissez faire. It is made for people of fundamentally differing views, and the accident of our finding certain opinions natural and familiar or novel and even shocking ought not to conclude our judgment upon the question whether statutes embodying them conflict with the Constitution of the United States.... I think the word liberty in the Fourteenth Amendment is perverted when it is held to prevent the natural outcome of a dominant opinion.

Holmes's posture in the "liberty of contract" cases excited many "progressive" observers of the Court. They thought his comments meant that he supported legislative actions that would improve the working conditions of industrial laborers. That was not so. Holmes believed that there was little legislatures could do to affect the "iron laws" of the industrial market. He simply thought, as he once put it, that if a majority of U.S. citizens wanted "to go to Hell, it is my job to help them do so." He distinguished between the principle of majority rule in a constitutional democracy, which he supported, and the wisdom of majority decisions, many of which he thought foolish. He was not the progressive or liberal judge some of his supporters made him out to be.

Holmes took the same approach to legislation that one might today consider repressive rather than progressive. An example was the 1927 case of *Buck* v. *Bell*. That case involved the constitutionality of a Virginia law that allowed for the sterilization of residents of state mental facilities if they were classified as "mental defectives." Carrie Buck, the daughter of a resident of the State Colony for Epileptics and the Feeble-Minded, was designated to be sterilized because she, as well as her mother, had been placed in the category of "mental defectives" and because she had given birth to an illegitimate child. Her sterilization was upheld by the highest state court in Virginia, but her lawyers challenged it on the ground that she had a constitutional right to "bodily integrity." Even though Carrie Buck and her family were residents of the State Colony only because other family members could not take care of them, even though there was no evidence that she was a "mental defective," and even though the decision to sterilize her was made because she had had an illegitimate child, Holmes upheld the Virginia statute and permitted the sterilization of Carrie Buck.

The principle by which Holmes protested against the invalidation of wages and hours legislation and upheld compulsory sterilization laws was the same: He did not believe that it was his job to invalidate legislation unless there was what he called "an overwhelming constitutional mandate," that is, unless the Constitution clearly forbid the legislation. As a judge in a constitutional democracy, he needed to avoid substituting what he thought was appropriate policy for what a majority thought was right or what the Constitution required.

A group of progressive intellectuals, however, who supported legislative reform efforts in the early 20th century, took Holmes's posture of deference to legislative action as sympathetic to their views and began to find him an attractive judicial figure in the years just before World War I. The year 1912, in fact, was a pivotal one in Holmes's career, not because of any important decisions he wrote but because it marked the beginning of a transformation in his reputation.

In 1912 Holmes was approaching the close of his first decade as a Supreme Court justice. He was 71 years old, and by December he could retire with a full pension. He seriously contemplated retirement; during his first 10 years on the Court he had remained relatively obscure, writing only an occasional opinion that was widely noticed. His dissent in *Lochner* v. *New York* was not yet thought of as a "classic," as it was later called.

But that year, a young graduate of Harvard Law School moved to Washington and presented a letter of introduction to Holmes from John Gray. Felix Frankfurter had graduated in 1906 and become a protégé of Henry Stimson, the U.S. attorney in New York at the time. When Stimson became head of the Bureau of Insular Affairs in the Taft administration, Frankfurter followed him to Washington. Shortly thereafter he contacted Holmes.

Frankfurter was connected to a circle of young progressive intellectuals, both lawyers and nonlawyers, who were committed to social reform, democratization of the processes of popular government, and economic regulation initiated and managed by elites. This group adopted Holmes as one of its heroes, basing their judgment, in part, on Holmes's dissents in the cases from *Lochner* to *Adkins,* which they read as support for progressive legislative efforts to regulate industrial labor relations. At the very time when Holmes seemed fated to remain an obscure judge, perhaps even to retire, he was suddenly rejuvenated by the realization that he had been recognized and was admired by a group of young men who might well be the wave of the political future. That recognition was the beginning of Holmes's becoming a historic American figure.

8

THE YANKEE FROM OLYMPUS

When Felix Frankfurter first made contact with Holmes, he had been living in Washington for a year. His residence was a large house on 19th Street owned by Robert Grosvenor Valentine, the commissioner of Indian affairs during the presidency of William Howard Taft. Valentine's house, known as the "House of Truth" by its residents, became a political and intellectual gathering place for progressive intellectuals in the years before and during World War I. Frankfurter and his associates were involved in and keenly concerned with Washington politics and larger issues of policy making, and they thought of themselves as political reformers. They invited public officials and other dignitaries, including Holmes, to the "House of Truth." Holmes, in turn, invited Frankfurter to visit him at his home, and the two began to engage in correspondence.

On March 8, 1912, Holmes turned 71, and Frankfurter wrote him a birthday note. "Your pipe *has* reached deep and permanently into the hearts of [many of us]," Frankfurter told Holmes. "[O]ur own striving has a richer meaning and a deeper significance from your being.... A long continued youth to you!" Holmes responded by saying:

The Supreme Court justices at a White House reception shortly after William Howard Taft's confirmation as chief justice. In front from left to right stand Louis Brandeis, John Clarke, Mahlon Pitney, Willis Van DeVanter, James McReynolds, William Day, Holmes, Joseph McKenna, and Taft.

It will be many years before you have occasion to know the happiness and encouragement that comes to an old man from the sympathy of the young. That, perhaps more than anything else, makes one feel as if one had not lived in vain, and counteracts the eternal gravitation toward melancholy and doubt. I am quite sincere in saying that you have done a great deal for me in that way and I send you my gratitude and thanks.

For at least the next decade Frankfurter's numerous letters to Holmes sounded similar themes: how much Frankfurter admired Holmes, what a privilege it was to be in his company or to communicate with him, and, above all, how "young" or "youthful" Holmes was and thus what an inspirational figure he was. Holmes's letters to Frankfurter were far less personal and more concerned with various intellectual matters, but they often conveyed how much "happiness and encouragement" Holmes had received in being made aware of the "sympathy of the young." From 1912 to 1932, when Holmes retired from the Court, Frankfurter became the chief publicist of Holmes as a "great" judge, first to his contemporaries, then to the legal profession at large, and ultimately to the general public.

From his base at the "House of Truth" Frankfurter made a number of friends and contacts among young men who shared his reformist political ideas and his engagement with what he called "big public issues." He introduced several of his associates to Holmes, and their reaction was similar to Frankfurter's: Holmes appeared to them as a man from another time who nonetheless could embrace the present, a remote, austere figure who nonetheless loved stimulating intellectual discussion. Moreover, as a judge Holmes appeared enlightened and progressive, one of the very few of his colleagues whose attitudes appeared "modern."

Some of Frankfurter's associates in Washington subsequently became influential through the formation of a popular journal of public affairs, *The New Republic.* Officially launched in 1914, it became a journal of mainstream progressive thought. The editorial staff included such early-20th-century political writers as Herbert Croly and Walter Lippmann. Legal contributors to *The New Republic*'s pages included Frankfurter himself and Harold Laski, an English political theorist whom Frankfurter had introduced to Holmes in 1912 and who became one of Holmes's great correspondence friends. *The New Republic,* for almost two decades after its founding, consistently wrote flattering editorials and columns on Holmes's opinions.

From his base at Harvard Law School, Felix Frankfurter participated in a great many activities involving constitutional law and national politics, including a long-standing campaign to lionize Holmes's reputation as a great Supreme Court justice and legal thinker.

In 1913, with Woodrow Wilson having defeated Taft for the presidency, Henry Stimson expected to be leaving the Bureau of Insular Affairs, and Frankfurter with him. In the summer of 1913 Frankfurter received an offer to join the faculty at Harvard Law School, where he had been an exceptional student. Harvard had recently named Roscoe Pound, a visible progressive scholar, to its faculty, and Frankfurter admired his work. Frankfurter consulted Holmes, who took the occasion to issue his comment about academic life being "half-life," but Frankfurter nonetheless accepted the position. Once at Harvard he continued his interest in constitutional law and the decisions of the Supreme Court, and in 1916 he organized a commemorative tribute to Holmes in the *Harvard Law Review,* recognizing Holmes's 75th birthday. This was the first time an American journal of legal scholarship had devoted an issue to the decisions of a Supreme Court justice. It was the first

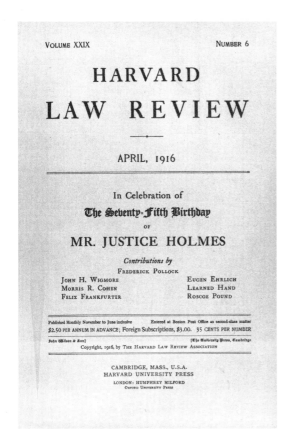

VOLUME XXIX   NUMBER 6

HARVARD
LAW REVIEW

APRIL, 1916

In Celebration of

The Seventy-Fifth Birthday

OF

MR. JUSTICE HOLMES

Contributions by

FREDERICK POLLOCK

JOHN H. WIGMORE	EUGEN EHRLICH
MORRIS R. COHEN	LEARNED HAND
FELIX FRANKFURTER	ROSCOE POUND

Published Monthly November to June inclusive   Entered at Boston Post Office as second-class matter
$2.50 PER ANNUM IN ADVANCE; Foreign Subscriptions, $3.00. 35 CENTS PER NUMBER

John Wilson & Son]   [The University Press, Cambridge

Copyright, 1916, by THE HARVARD LAW REVIEW ASSOCIATION

CAMBRIDGE, MASS., U.S.A.
HARVARD UNIVERSITY PRESS
LONDON: HUMPHREY MILFORD
Oxford University Press

The Harvard Law Review *was the first journal of its kind to honor a Supreme Court justice when it devoted an entire issue to Holmes's decisions in April 1916.*

signal to the legal community that Holmes was a judge of distinction.

Meanwhile Frankfurter, Laski (who began teaching in the Harvard political science department in 1916), and a young assistant professor at Harvard Law School named Zechariah Chafee began to take an interest in free-speech issues and eventually drew Holmes into their conversation. The entrance of the United States into World War I and the Bolshevik Revolution in Russia had given a new meaning to the concept of sedition, or subversive speech. After more than a century in which there had been no federal laws passed against speech tending to undermine the authority of the government, Congress passed two statutes in 1917 and 1918, the Espionage Act and the Sedition Act, that provided criminal penalties for speech which interfered with the war effort or attempted to undermine the authority of the U.S. government.

Although Congress had not passed any legislation restricting speech since the Alien and Sedition Acts of 1798 (which were never enforced), several states had passed laws restricting various forms of expression, such as criticism of public officials or expression that was obscene, libelous (false and damaging), blasphemous (critical of religious symbols), or offensive. Very few of these laws were challenged in cases before the Supreme Court. Although the 1st Amendment states that "Congress shall make no law abridging freedom of speech," the amendment was not thought to apply to the states. In addition, orthodox legal thinking about free-speech issues in the 19th century followed the position of the British legal scholar, Sir William Blackstone. In his influential *Commentaries on the Law of England* (1765–69), Blackstone wrote that freedom of speech consisted only in protection from "previous restraints" (that is, government censorship). Blackstone felt that subversive or otherwise inappropriate expressions, once published, could be punished.

Holmes had himself written two opinions on the Supreme Court, *Patterson* v. *Colorado* (1907) and *Fox* v. *Washington* (1915), in which he rejected free-speech challenges to state legislation and suggested that he endorsed Blackstone's position. And in 1919, when the first challenges to the Espionage Act of 1917 came to the Supreme Court, Holmes wrote unanimous opinions in all of the cases upholding convictions under the act. In one of the cases, however, he modified his earlier views and set forth an apparently new judicial test for determining when an act of Congress restricting speech violated the 1st Amendment.

The case was *Schenck* v. *United States,* in which some officials of the American Socialist party, which criticized war as a means of resolving disputes, were convicted under the Espionage Act for distributing circulars to men who had been drafted into the army. The circulars stated that conscription, or the mandatory drafting of soldiers by the government, was a "monstrous wrong against humanity in the interest of Wall Street's chosen few."

Holmes, in his majority opinion, said that the 1st Amendment's protection of speech was "not confined to previous restraints." This was a departure from his earlier free-speech opinions for the Court. He then proposed a test for determining whether a federal statute that sought to make subversive speech criminal violated the 1st Amendment. "The question in every case," he wrote, "is whether the words used are used in such circumstances and of such a nature as to create a clear and present danger that they will bring about the substantive evils that Congress had a right to prevent." In the *Schenck* case, Holmes reasoned, the distribution of leaflets attacking the draft to soldiers who had just been drafted could be said to produce a "clear and present danger": Soldiers reading them might resist being conscripted into military service, a response that if undertaken by enough soldiers might undermine U.S. participation in World War I, a "substantive evil" that Congress surely "had a right to prevent."

In his opinion in *Schenck,* Holmes appeared to be taking free-speech challenges more seriously than he had in previous Supreme Court decisions. But he did not use the "clear and present danger" test for subversive speech in all his opinions after *Schenck.* One case involved Eugene Debs, the Socialist party candidate for President in 1912, who had made a speech supporting the Socialist party platform, which included a general condemnation of war. Debs

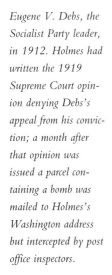

Eugene V. Debs, the Socialist Party leader, in 1912. Holmes had written the 1919 Supreme Court opinion denying Debs's appeal from his conviction; a month after that opinion was issued a parcel containing a bomb was mailed to Holmes's Washington address but intercepted by post office inspectors.

praised three "loyal comrades" who were in jail for "aiding and abetting another in failing to register for the draft." He added, "I abhor war. I would oppose the war if I stood alone" and said that he "had to be prudent and might not be able to say all he thought" about his friends' efforts to avoid the draft. He was convicted under the Espionage Act.

Holmes upheld Debs's conviction in a 1919 Supreme Court case. He did not mention his "clear and present danger" test, and it is hard to see how Debs's statement of his general opposition to war, and his hints that he would like to say more about the activities of his comrades, amounted to creating a clear and present danger that would undermine the recruiting efforts for World War I. Presumably Debs's audience, which consisted of Socialist party supporters, would not have been in a position to obstruct the recruiting service simply by publicizing Debs's general opposition to war.

Debs's conviction and Holmes's opinion were criticized in a 1919 article in *The New Republic* by Ernst Freund, a professor at the University of Chicago School of Law. Freund argued that by convicting Debs in a situation where there was "nothing to show actual obstruction or an attempt to interfere with any of the recruitment process," the jury had been "guessing" at the "tendency and possible effect" of Debs's comments. This did not seem consistent with the "clear and present danger" requirement of *Schenck* and, in Freund's view, made "the right of free speech a precarious gift," subject to the whims of juries.

Freund's article came to the attention of Holmes, who also received what he called "stupid letters of protest" against the *Debs* decision. Holmes's wrote to several friends that he was sorry that the government had brought charges against Schenck and Debs, now that the war had ended, and he hoped that Debs would be pardoned (he eventually was). He said that Chief Justice White had chosen him to write the opinions in the Espionage Act cases because he was known to be the justice most sympathetic to free-speech claims on the Court. At the same time he insisted that both Schenck and Debs had been properly convicted.

These two cases, together with a third Espionage Act case in which Holmes also sustained a conviction, were handed down in the spring of 1919. In May of that year Freund's criticism of the *Debs* opinion appeared, and around the same time newspapers revealed that Holmes had been on a list of people who were scheduled to receive bombs in the mail. Packages containing bombs were found on April 30, 1919, in a New York City post office, where they had been set aside for insufficient postage. The bombs were timed to explode on May 1, the second anniversary of the Bolshevik Revolution in Russia. On being informed that he was one of the targets of the bombs, Holmes wrote Harold Laski that "I suppose it was the Debs incident that secured me the honor."

In June 1919 Zechariah Chafee published an article in the *Harvard Law Review* on free speech. Chafee's article considered Holmes's Espionage Act decisions and argued that they abandoned Blackstone's view that protection for free speech should be limited to freedom from prior censorship. At the same time, he claimed, Holmes's decisions created a new test for determining whether speech should be protected—a test that balanced the social interest in public safety against the social interest in the "discovery and spread of truth on matters of general concern." Chafee thought that Holmes's "clear and present danger" test would be a good one for future cases because it provided an opportunity for this balancing. But he criticized Holmes for not "concentrating his great abilities on fixing the line" between protected and unprotected speech under "clear and present danger" and for not "emphasizing the social interest behind free speech." Chafee implied that although Holmes's test in *Schenck* was promising, he had not followed through by applying it rigorously in *Debs*.

In late July 1919 Laski invited Holmes, who was staying in his summer house at Beverly Farms, Massachusetts, to have tea with him at Cambridge to meet Zechariah Chafee and discuss free-speech issues. After the meeting Chafee wrote a friend that he had failed to convince Holmes that he had missed an opportunity in his Espionage Act decisions to articulate the principles behind greater protection for speech. But Chafee was wrong: Holmes had come to appreciate Chafee's position.

In November 1919 the Supreme Court decided another free-speech case, *Abrams* v. *United States.* It involved a group of Russian immigrants, supporters of the Bolshevik Revolution, who threw some leaflets out of an apartment window onto a street where there was a factory that made ammunition for the military. The leaflets criticized President Woodrow Wilson's decision to send U.S. troops into Russia to support forces fighting the Bolsheviks. They also urged the factory workers, some of whom were Russian immigrants, to go on a general strike because the weapons the factory was producing would end up being used against the Bolsheviks. The authors of the leaflets were convicted under the Sedition Act of 1918, which had amended the Espionage Act of 1917 to make it a crime not only to obstruct the recruitment of troops but to "urge … any curtailment of production … with intent to cripple … the United States in the prosecution of the war." Although the authors of the leaflets were not interested in affecting the war with Germany, their distribution of the leaflets had taken place while that war was still going on.

A majority of the Supreme Court upheld the conviction of the authors of the leaflets in the *Abrams* case. Justice John Clarke, who wrote the majority opinion, reasoned that the case was similar to *Debs* in that general opposition to war could, under the circumstances, encourage specific opposition to a particular war. The statements had that "probable effect," Clarke concluded. Although he considered the *Schenck* case a precedent, he did not mention the "clear and present danger" test.

Holmes issued a dissent in the *Abrams* case, which identified him with a position on free speech close to that which Chafee had taken in his June 1919 article. He reaffirmed, and restated, the importance of the "clear and present danger" test for speech cases, saying that *Schenck* and *Debs* stood for the principle that "the United States constitutionally may punish speech that produces or is intended to produce a clear and imminent danger that it will bring about forthwith certain substantive evils that the United States constitutionally may seek to prevent." In *Schenck* Holmes had used the term "present danger"; he now said "imminent danger." In *Schenck* he had referred to "substantive evils that Congress has a right to prevent"; that phrase, in his *Abrams* dissent, became "certain substantive evils that the United States constitutionally may seek to prevent." The *Schenck* test suggested that whenever the federal government could identify a "substantive evil" that it obviously had power to oppose, it could restrict speech that had some tendency to further that evil. Holmes's restatement of that test in *Abrams* appeared to place a much stronger burden on the federal government to justify restricting speech. The connection between the speech and the "evil" had to be "imminent," and the evil had to be one that—despite the 1st Amendment's instructions that Congress should make "no law" abridging the freedom of speech—the government could *constitutionally* seek to prevent.

Thus Holmes gave his "clear and present danger" test for speech cases much more bite in his *Abrams* dissent. In addition, he provided a principle for the protection of free speech, and that principle turned out to be precisely the one Chafee had offered in his *Harvard Law Review* article. In particularly vivid and memorable language, Holmes said:

> When men have realized that time has upset many fighting faiths, they may come to believe even

more than they believe the very foundations of their own conduct that the ultimate good desired is better reached by free trade in ideas—that the best test of truth is the power of the thought to get itself accepted in the competition of the market, and that truth is the only ground upon which their wishes safely can be carried out.

Having articulated the principle of "free trade in ideas" as part of the "search for truth," Holmes then tied that principle to the U.S. Constitution:

> That at any rate is the theory of our Constitution. It is an experiment, as all life is an experiment.... While that experiment is part of our system I think that we should be eternally vigilant against attempts to check the expression of opinions that we loathe ... unless they so imminently threaten immediate interference with the lawful and pressing purposes of the law that an immediate check is required to save the country.

Then Holmes tied this theory of the Constitution back to his "clear and present danger" test:

> Only the emergency that makes it imminently dangerous to leave the correction of evil counsels to time warrants making any exception to the sweeping command, "Congress shall make no law ... abridging the freedom of speech."

The perspective on free-speech issues that Holmes urged in his *Abrams* dissent was one designed to get his readers to appreciate, on the one hand, the great significance of protection for freedom of speech in U.S. constitutional democracy and, on the other, the relatively harmless, trivial quality of the speech that the government sought to make criminal in *Abrams*. Holmes was suggesting that, far from being any immediate threat to public safety, the leaflets distributed by the defendants in *Abrams* were so obviously foolish and wrongheaded that they would instantly encourage others to respond with a more balanced and accurate assessment of the connection between the operations at one munitions factory and the progress of the Bolshevik Revolution. Thus the leaflets, which Holmes characterized as "silly" products of a "creed of ignorance and immaturity," actually promoted the search for truth in discussions of public affairs.

Progressive commentators praised Holmes's *Abrams* dissent. Harold Laski wrote to Holmes that "amongst the many opinions of yours that I have read, none seems to me superior either in nobility of outlook, [or] in dignity of phrasing." *The New Republic* produced an editorial highly critical of the majority opinion in *Abrams* and endorsed Holmes's dissent. And Chafee, in another *Harvard Law Review* article on the case, spoke of "Justice Holmes's magnificent exposition of the philosophic basis" of the 1st Amendment and suggested that the dissent would "carry great weight as an interpretation of the First Amendment, because it is only an elaboration of the principle laid down by him with the backing of a unanimous court in *Schenck* v. *United States*." Chafee concluded that Holmes's "clear and present danger" test could now be taken as "marking the true limit of governmental interference with speech and writing under our Constitution."

Of course Chafee was not exactly accurate in those conclusions. Although Holmes had introduced the "clear and present danger" test in *Schenck,* he had not followed it at all in *Debs.* The Court majority in *Abrams,* although reaffirming that the *Schenck* principles governed that case, had certainly not employed the kind of rephrased "clear and present danger" test that Holmes used in his dissent. And for the remainder of Holmes's career, only he and Justice Louis Brandeis, who joined Holmes's dissenting opinion in *Abrams,* endorsed a vigorous "clear and present danger" test. A majority of the Court did not adopt the "clear and present danger" test as its standard for evaluating free-speech claims until after 1937, five years after Holmes's retirement and two years after his death.

Holmes continued to dissent in several free-speech cases for the balance of his career and continued to receive acclaim from many academic commentators for doing so. His free-speech opinions from *Abrams* on represented a not altogether consistent but growing commitment to the principle of protection for speech in a democratic society. Although in some of those opinions he continued to stress that speech should be protected primarily because it contributed to the spread of truthful information about public issues, in others he seemed to endorse "the principle of free thought—not free thought for those who agree with us but freedom for the thought that we hate," as he stated in the 1929 case of *United States* v. *Schwimmer.* By the end of his career he seemed to hold a view that speech was a constitutional "liberty" that judges should protect even in the face of decisions by legislative majorities to restrict it. This view was the reverse of the position of deference that Holmes had taken in the "liberty of contract" cases, in which he had voted to uphold the decisions of legislative majorities that restricted individual choices in the marketplace.

Such a stance did not affect the growth of Holmes's progressive reputation. On the contrary, his identification with opinions arguing for expanded protection for freedom of speech helped cement his image as a tolerant, liberal judge, one who had transcended the prejudices of his class to support the claims of people such as the Russian immigrants in *Abrams.* This was another misreading of Holmes's sensibility. One of the reasons that he tolerated these kinds of expressions was that he had so little respect for the messages being communicated. He thought them foolish and "immature" and unlikely to have much influence.

In the years between Holmes's 75th birthday and his retirement from the Supreme Court at the age of 90— the years in which he produced all of his major free-speech opinions—Holmes's supporters launched an intellectual campaign to bring him and his writings to the attention of the general public. Frankfurter followed up his 1916 birthday tribute in the *Harvard Law Review* with an article in 1923 celebrating "Twenty Years of Mr. Justice Holmes's Constitutional Opinions." In the meantime, as Harold Laski put it, Frankfurter had "been teaching the growing youth" that opinions such as Holmes's dissent in *Lochner* "have really got a philosophy in them."

In the summer of 1919 Laski had proposed to Holmes that he collect some of his speeches and articles into a book, and Holmes sent him a list of speeches and articles that might be included. Eventually *Collected Legal Papers* was published in November 1920. It was generously reviewed in *The New Republic, The Nation,* the *Boston Evening Transcript,* and by Roscoe Pound, the dean of Harvard Law School, in the *Harvard Law Review.*

In the 1920s Holmes's reputation began to expand beyond legal circles to include the general public. In 1924 he received the Roosevelt (now Presidential) Medal of Freedom from President Calvin Coolidge for "distinguished service to the American people." Two years later Elizabeth Shipley Sergeant wrote an article for *The New Republic* that appeared in December 1926, when Holmes was 85 years old. Previous commentary on Holmes in *The New Republic* had been confined to his judicial opinions, but the Sergeant article was a portrait of Holmes the man. Sergeant had set out to interview Fanny Holmes as well, but over the course of talks with Sergeant, Fanny concluded that she disliked the young woman and demanded that all references to herself in the article be deleted.

Sergeant's article opened with the sentence, "Here is a Yankee, strayed from Olympus." Like the progressives who had discovered him earlier, Sergeant portrayed Holmes as a figure from another time who was somehow modern. He was, Sergeant wrote, a descendant of "the natural Puritan aristocracy," a "gallant gentleman of old New England." But he was at the same time a man who thought of life as "a rich but responsible adventure," whose extraordinary life span and continued vitality made him "the most romantic of contemporary Americans." In the phrase "Yankee, strayed from Olympus" Sergeant sought to capture the dual fascination of Holmes for early-20th-century Americans: He was, on the one hand, a figure so exalted and ancient as to be Olympian and, on the other, a "Yankee" living in the modern world.

At the very end of Holmes's career on the Court, editions of his opinions designed for the general public began to appear. Alfred Lief, a journalist, edited a volume entitled *The Dissenting Opinions of Mr. Justice Holmes* in 1929, followed in 1931 by *Representative Opinions of Mr. Justice Holmes.* Most of the opinions Lief chose were edited with an eye for memorable passages, passages that sometimes were noteworthy more for their literary qualities than for their legal arguments. In addition, the volumes gave the impression that Holmes quite frequently dissented in Supreme Court cases, as if he were at odds with the majority of his colleagues most of the time. This was not the case: Several other justices who served on the Court with Holmes wrote more dissents than he did, and Holmes's positions were often misunderstood by his admirers.

But the Lief volumes, another *Harvard Law Review* tribute on Holmes's 90th birthday, and a popular 1932 biography by Silas Bent (Holmes called it "harmless" and indicated that he had done his best to forestall future biographies by destroying any revealing papers he could find) introduced a larger audience of Americans to Holmes's distinctive style. By the third decade of the 20th century, that style was considered both accessible and appealing. The very qualities—brevity, ambiguity, a tendency toward rhetorical flourishes—that earlier commentators had criticized as "brilliant but not sound" now made Holmes appear as a judge whose writing the general public could appreciate. Even legal commentators began to speak favorably of Holmes's judicial style.

A typical example of Holmes's writing appears in his decision of a case about whether evidence obtained by illegal wiretapping could be admitted against a defendant in a criminal prosecution:

> There is no body of precedents by which we are bound, and which confines us to logical deduction from established rules. Therefore we must consider the two objects of desire, both of which we cannot have, and make up our minds which to choose. It is desirable that criminals should be detected, and to that end that all available evidence should be used. It is also desirable that the government should not itself foster and pay for other crimes, when they are the means by which the evidence is to be obtained.... We have to choose, and for my part I think it a less evil that some criminals should escape than that the government should play an ignoble part.

Some of the pronouncements in Holmes's opinions are not confined to law but range beyond it to philosophy or metaphysics. Especially to a reader without specialized legal training, the pronouncement, rather than its application, is the more memorable part of the opinion.

In a case in which a police officer in New Bedford, Massachusetts, was fired for soliciting money for a political cause, Holmes wrote that "a policeman may have a constitutional right to talk politics, but he has no constitutional right to be a policeman." This looks like a pronouncement that everyone would agree with. We assume that the 1st Amendment gives citizens a "constitutional right to talk politics," the freedom to express political views, even if they are not shared by others. We also assume that holding the job of a policeman, like holding any job, is not something that a person has a "constitutional right" to hold.

But the way in which Holmes uses his pronouncement is misleading. He follows it up by saying, "There are few employments for hire in which the servant does not agree to suspend his constitutional right of free speech." That statement is not accurate as a general proposition. For example, although an employee of a factory may agree not to boost publicly the competition and thereby gives up that right to free speech, he does not give up the right to other speech. The employee has an interest in not aiding the competition, but he has no reason not to express other ideas that his boss perhaps does not support.

In the New Bedford case the policeman was soliciting money for a political campaign in which his office was not directly involved. He was discharged because the mayor did not want officials of the city to appear as if they were partisan. Suppose, however, that the policeman had voted in a city election, or contributed to the campaign of one of the candidates, without publicizing those actions on his job. Could he be fired? If not, one might say that he had a "constitutional right to be a policeman without being forced to give up his right to vote." In other words, just because an employer has the right to choose employees, that employer does not have the right to attach unconstitutional conditions to the employment.

Holmes's pronouncement that a policeman has a constitutional right to talk politics but not to be a policeman was an oversimplification. But the pronouncement captured an important distinction between constitutional rights and economic opportunities, and it articulated that distinction in language that many different kinds of readers could understand.

Over and over in his opinions Holmes was able to communicate through such generalized pronouncements, which were often helpful in showing readers what lay at "the bottom" of the case Holmes was deciding: the policy choices he and his fellow judges were making and the philosophical basis of the principles they were laying down. Such pronouncements also often provided the reader with a phrase that was easy to remember because of its arresting language and memorable imagery. "A word is not a crystal, transparent and unchanged; it is the skin of a living thought" is an example of one of the numerous epigrams Holmes wrote that transcend the cases in which he wrote them.

In the years after his death more and more of Holmes's correspondence became available to the general public, as collections of his letters were extracted from his private papers and from correspondence kept by his friends. Those members of the public that had become interested in Holmes as a judge who could turn memorable phrases had their interest widened by Holmes as a letter writer. In his private correspondence, Holmes spoke even more directly to the average reader. He wrote about politics, economics, philosophy, and books, as well as law or legal issues. He became, in his capacity as a memorable writer and thinker, a personage equivalent to that of his father.

SHOCKING SPEECH

Holmes believed that most "shocking" speech amounted to foolish statements by irrational or poorly educated people, and the best remedy to prevent such speech from gaining any influence was to let it into the public domain, where its foolishness would quickly be recognized. In his dissents in free speech cases he often emphasized the silly, immature, or irrational quality of the expressions he believed deserved constitutional protection. Holmes's views on free speech were also often misunderstood, as this 1925 letter to his young British friend Lewis Einstein suggests.

Beverly Farms, July 11, 1925

Dear Einstein,

I was just writing a day or two ago to a friend who repeated a criticism of my opinions that they might be literature but were not the proper form of judicial expression. My notion was that longwinded expositions of the obvious were as out of place in opinions as elsewhere. This however is not intended as a hit at the judgment of the majority in the Gitlow case [*Gitlow* v. *New York* (1925), in which Holmes had dissented from a Court decision upholding a New York law banning speech advocating "overthrow of the government," as applied to a publication calling for mass strikes]. I had my whack at free speech some years ago in the case of one Abrams, and therefore [in his *Gitlow* dissent] did no more than lean on that.... To show the ardor of the writer is not a sufficient reason for judging him. I regarded my view as simply upholding the right of a donkey to drool. But the usual notion is that you are free to say what you like if you don't shock me. Of course the value of the constitutional right is only when you do shock people....

Sincerely yours,
O. W. Holmes

9

TOWARD MELANCHOLY: THE RETIREMENT YEARS

Among the many remarkable things about Holmes's 90th-birthday radio address was the physical and mental condition of the man who wrote and spoke it. Today most public figures, including Supreme Court justices, have help in writing their speeches, opinions, or other public pronouncements. Not only did Holmes write all of his opinions in 50 years as a judge, but he wrote all his speeches, addresses, essays, scholarly articles, and *The Common Law*. He wrote all his voluminous letters, of course, and when he was asked to make a brief speech on the radio, he wrote that. The long-hand draft of that speech reveals that he intended it to take up no more than one page; he made only a few corrections to the original sentences he wrote. At 90 his ability to create memorable prose had not diminished.

From the time he returned to Boston with his third war wound in 1863 to his 90th birthday, Holmes had been in very good health. He had learned to ride horseback in the Civil War and took up bicycle riding in his 50s, when two-wheel bicycles became popular, but he did not participate in athletics and did not mention any regular forms of exercise in his correspondence. He was accustomed to reg-

In his study at home in Washington, D.C., Holmes wrote his Supreme Court opinions and his volu-minous correspondence. The leather chair next to his desk was his favorite reading spot, and the book-shelves were filled with the reports of judicial opinions, many of which he had authored.

ularly walking the two miles from his home on Eye Street to the Capitol to attend Supreme Court arguments. Daily walking was perhaps part of his routine, as it was for most 19th-century Americans. He smoked cigars, limiting himself to one a day, and drank wine with his dinner. He was careful about his health and cautioned his younger friends "not to run the motor too hard."

In 1922, when he was 81, Holmes was hospitalized to treat an inflamed prostate gland. Doctors successfully operated on Holmes in the second week of July, but given the surgical techniques of the time and his age, convalescence was expected to be slow.

When the Supreme Court opened its 1922 term in October, Holmes was able to take his seat, but he moved around with difficulty, and an elevator had been installed in his house to help him get about. In January he reported to Nina Gray that he was "still shaky on my legs—and get out of the car as if I were an old man." By the summer of 1923, however, he had regained his strength.

Between 1923 and his 90th birthday Holmes had no additional serious illnesses. His life, by the 1920s, had settled into a routine that included comparatively few social engagements and a great deal of reading and correspondence. He enjoyed being driven in a car that Fanny had convinced him to buy, but he never learned to drive himself. In 1927 he wrote a unanimous opinion for the Court in a case, *Baltimore & Ohio Railroad* v. *Goodman,* that laid down an impractical set of rules for car drivers when they approached railroad crossings: Drivers must stop their cars and look for a train, even getting out of the car if necessary. The case was overruled seven years later by the Court, and Justice Benjamin Cardozo pointed out that the proper conduct of drivers varied so dramatically with circumstances that laying down rules in advance was probably futile.

Holmes's routine during the 1920s also included regular companionship with his current secretary (what would today be called a law clerk) and with Fanny. His secretaries did almost no legal research, their job as researchers consisting mainly of retrieving books or finding citations for Holmes to use when he was writing opinions. The secretary's primary duty was to be an intellectual companion for Holmes, reading books with him, discussing ideas, and serving as a sounding board for his views. On most evenings Fanny would read aloud to Wendell while he played solitaire, and she continued to take care of domestic arrangements, along with household servants.

Because Fanny was reclusive and did not like publicity, little is known about the state of her health or her life after she and her husband moved to Washington. In Beverly Farms, where they went for the summer, Fanny was no more active socially than she had been in Boston or Washington: A visitor to their summer house reported that she kept all the shutters and curtains drawn.

In the fall of 1928 Fanny, at age 88, fell in the house on Eye Street on three separate occasions and was bedridden each time. She also contracted a series of viruses that left her in a relatively weak condition. In April 1929 she suffered another fall, this time breaking her hip. It was set in a plaster cast, and Fanny was immobilized; pneumonia eventually set in. Fanny Holmes died on April 30.

Holmes, as a Civil War veteran, was entitled to a burial plot in Arlington National Cemetery, and Fanny was buried there. Holmes had purchased a joint gravestone. On it he had inscribed, "Oliver Wendell Holmes, Brevet Colonel & Captain, 20th Mass. Volunteers Infantry, Justice Supreme

Holmes with John Knox, a friend of Alger Hiss, Holmes's law clerk for the 1929–30 term. Hiss took the picture in September 1930, at Beverly Farms, Massachusetts, Holmes's summer home. Holmes was to turn 90 the following March; Hiss was to be the last survivor of Holmes's law clerks, dying in 1996.

Court of United States," along with the month and year of his birth. Fanny's gravestone said, "His Wife, Fanny B. Holmes, Dec. 1840, April 30, 1929." Obituaries in the *Washington Post* and *Boston Globe* did not mention Fanny by name, referring to her as "Justice Holmes's Wife." Wendell and Fanny had been married for 57 years at the time of her death. Holmes wrote that her death "seems like the beginning of my own." But at the same time he made it clear to Chief Justice William Howard Taft that he had no intention of resigning from the Court. He told Felix Frankfurter that his judicial work seemed "to be done at a separate chamber of one's being—unaffected by any troubles." The day Fanny died he wrote an opinion and sent it to Taft.

Holmes's secretaries now took a more active role in his private life—balancing his checkbook, paying his bills, and reading to him in the evenings. Although Holmes called each of his secretaries "sonny" and did not seem to distinguish one clearly from another in the late stages of his tenure on the Court, they were important people in his life, and they filled, in part, the void that Fanny left.

Holmes continued his work on the Court without apparent difficulty up until his 90 birthday. That summer, however, he arrived at Beverly Farms feeling tired, although by August he wrote to Nina Gray that he was feeling better. Shortly after that letter he seems to have had a mild stroke or heart attack. He later referred to the incident as "a sort of cave in" that left him considerably fatigued and unable to grip a pen without difficulty. His correspondence dwindled to an occasional note, and he dictated some letters. His bedroom in Beverly Farms was moved to the first floor, and on September 22 he wrote Nina Gray that the summer had been "disappointing in my being ill most of the time." He added, however, that he planned to resume his work on the Court that October.

By the October 1931 term Holmes's secretary and his judicial colleagues had begun to be concerned about his

"I Have Had My Reward"

After Fanny's death, Holmes made it clear to Chief Justice Taft that he did not intend to retire from the Court. In fact, he completed an opinion the day she died. This letter to Lewis Einstein, dated June 1929, suggests that while he recognized that Fanny's death, at 89, was a foreshadowing of his own, he was determined to go on working and living as long as he could. Although the letter has some comments about Fanny, emphasizing her reclusiveness and her sensitivity to criticism, it is mainly about Holmes, and its message, despite Holmes's satisfaction with his accomplishments, is "don't write me off yet."

My affectionate thanks for your kind and feeling letter. It was better that my wife should die than live in suffering and pain which I am sure was the alternative. I think too that it was better that she should die before I do; she was of the same age as I, and I think would have been more at a loss than I am if left alone. I like solitude with intermissions, but she was almost a recluse. I have my work and a fair number of people whom I like to see. She shocked Gifford Pinchot [director of the U.S. Forest Service] once by saying "I have no friends"; and it was true that there was no one except me with whom she was very intimate. Things hurt her that I didn't mind. We have a lovely spot at Arlington where she lies.

I may last even a year or two; but my work is done, though.... I shouldn't mind writing decisions in my ninetieth year and still better at ninety. I have had my reward, especially in these last years in the form of letters and articles. I wrote to a man yesterday, who had said super-superlative things, that if the devil came round the corner and said: You and I know that that isn't true, I should believe him. Still so long as he didn't appear in person, such letters kept alive my hope that I had lived my dream.

capacity to do his work. His secretary, Chapman Rose, later described the fall of 1931 as

> a period of considerable worry because the way in which his age affected him was ... an increasing fatigue. During the latter part of the day he would be very good and it was hard to imagine his ever having been better, during the hours when he was vigorous. But a pall would descend, sometimes earlier, sometimes later.... The attention span had gone without depriving him of the drive that he always had to finish any unfinished business.... So it was getting more difficult to prevent him from really exhausting himself and I remember ... being considerably concerned about what if anything ought to be done.

In addition to getting tired while attempting to keep up with his work, Holmes was beginning to doze during the Court's oral arguments. Some of the other justices became concerned that Holmes might embarrass himself in Court or in some other public setting.

Given Holmes's extraordinary longevity and great fame, in addition to his remarkable intellectual powers, the discussion of retirement with him was a particularly delicate matter. After consulting with Louis Brandeis, however, Chief Justice Charles Evans Hughes decided to bring up the issue with Holmes. He made an appointment to meet with him on Sunday morning, January 12, 1932. In a brief conversation, Hughes suggested to Holmes that work was becoming too physically demanding for him and told him that his colleagues were concerned about his health. Holmes understood that Hughes was proposing that he retire, and Holmes wrote his resignation letter on the spot. In it he said that "the condition of my health makes it a duty to break off connections that I cannot leave without deep regret." According to Chapman Rose, Hughes left the house "with tears streaming down his face." Holmes, however, was "then and thereafter totally stoic" about his resignation, according to Rose, showing "no expression of emotion one way or another." "The time has come," he added, "and I bow to the inevitable."

Holmes's resignation from the Court did not fundamentally change his routine, but it left a great gap in his life. His last years were marked by relative comfort, financial security, and the continued companionship of his secretaries and friends, but at the same time he felt what he had once called a "gravitation toward melancholy and doubt" that was directly related to his retirement.

Chapman Rose stayed on as Holmes's secretary through the summer of 1932, and in September a new secretary, Donald Hiss, began work. Many years later Hiss described the routine he and Holmes followed, which was to be the same for the remainder of Holmes's life.

Charles Evans Hughes served as chief justice of the United States from 1930 to 1941. Hughes had been among the speakers praising Holmes on his 90th birthday; less than a year later, on Sunday, January 12, 1932, Hughes visited Holmes at his home and persuaded him to retire from the Court.

I arrived at nine o'clock and worked a seven-day week. I took care of bills, other matters of immediate concern, certain household affairs, and any letters he received…. I'd start the day by asking if he wanted me to read to him, or whether he wanted to look at some of his engravings or do other things on his own. Usually about 11:30 I would read to him, and the selection [of a book to read] was a joint effort…. His tastes varied from [philosophy and art history to suspense novels]. Occasionally he would observe, "Sonny, at ninety-one, one outlives duty. Let's read E. Phillips Oppenheim [a suspense novelist]." He was very fond of the lighter things. But the reading and the discussion were always varied.

At one o'clock we had lunch down in the dining room. His visitors ranged from [the novelist] Owen Wister, Benjamin Cardozo [who had replaced Holmes on the Supreme Court] ... to Felix Frankfurter, but most of the time we lunched alone. After lunch he would go upstairs and drop off for a few minutes' nap, sometimes while I read to him and other times without my reading to him. We always took a drive in the afternoon.... He always wore his swallowtail coat when he was driving. When he came in he had an old alpaca coat that he shifted to.

After the drive we would read. At six o'clock I would leave and at seven o'clock he would have his supper, with Mary Donnellan [his housekeeper] in attendance. Except for a few instances when old friends were in town, he dined alone. I would come back at 8:30 and read to him for an hour or so. This was the general routine, interspersed frequently with discussion of what we were reading or of almost any subject, because his interests were extremely wide. There was nothing that did not interest him except athletics.

Before his retirement Holmes had occupied his hours away from the Court in precisely the same manner: reading books, writing letters, taking drives, and discussing ideas with his secretaries. He had received some visitors at lunch and occasionally at dinner but had not participated in any other social engagements. But of course he had also devoted a significant part of his day to his work on the Court. It was that work that energized him and enabled him to ward off the aging process.

After his retirement, with no duties on the Court to contemplate, the habits that Holmes had developed exposed the solitary quality of his life. His routine had been designed to conserve his physical and mental strength for his work on the Court; now, instead of being a respite from his labors as a judge, it was the center of his life. Holmes did not feel as fulfilled in retirement as might have been expected from someone of his considerable accomplishments. Although scholars as well as the general public continued to appreciate his work, and his reputation as a "great" judge remained in place, Holmes did not appear to take much satisfaction from his fame. "Old men of achievement," Frankfurter wrote in a memorandum recording his impressions after a conversation with Holmes, "usually live on the juice of their achievements. Not O.W.H. His skepticism is so profound that he is skeptical … of the importance of his own significance and so gets no warming and soothing comfort from dwelling on and in his past."

Holmes had relied on himself and on his "power of work" for so long that when his work was finally over, he looked around and saw very little else that could give him comfort. He had sought recognition, but now that it was detached from his work, it seemed fleeting and insignificant. He had only a few intimate friends and had outlived nearly all of them. He had no children, and his remaining close friends were still occupied with their professions or lived far away. After more than 90 years he was essentially alone.

But Holmes did not give up life easily. The three years and two months between his retirement and his death on March 6, 1935, two days before his 94th birthday, were a slow, gradual slide into what he called "the final oblivion." He was not seriously ill again, although he continued to feel the effects of his 1931 "cave in." He continued to follow the routine described by Donald Hiss with a new secretary every September.

On February 23, 1935, Holmes and his secretary, James Rowe, went for their daily drive. The weather was raw, and the next morning Holmes developed a cold. It progressed into bronchial pneumonia, a serious condition, especially for someone of Holmes's age at a time when antibiotics were not available. By the end of the month newspapers

A bugler blows taps at Holmes's funeral, March 8, 1935, which would have been his 94th birthday. A mixture of rain and sleet fell during the funeral service, and as Holmes's casket was carried to his grave site at Arlington National Cemetery, his housekeeper, Mary Donellan, remarked, "Soldiers don't mind the rain."

were reporting that Holmes was seriously ill. Several of his former secretaries came to visit him, as did Frankfurter and several of the justices of the Supreme Court. He was placed in an oxygen tent on March 3 and died on the morning of March 6, "more peacefully," his doctor reported, "than anyone I've ever seen." His funeral was held on March 8, with the justices of the Supreme Court as honorary pallbearers. After the funeral Holmes's casket was transported to Arlington National Cemetery, where President Franklin Roosevelt met the procession.

Holmes's estate was valued at more than $568,000, which made him a wealthy man for his times. One of his biographers, John Monagan, has speculated that $500,000 in 1935 dollars would be close to $5 million today. Very little of the income Holmes earned went in taxes to the government: Until 1913 there was no income tax, and

between that year and 1935 income taxes ranged from 1 to 7 percent of a person's annual income. Holmes's salary as a Supreme Court justice had gone from about $12,000 a year when he was named to the Court in 1902 to $20,000 on his retirement, and his retirement pension was equal to his salary. Most of his estate was in investments, made primarily with money he had inherited from his father, some of whose literary efforts had been quite profitable.

When Holmes's estate was distributed, his nephew received $100,000; two cousins, a total of $35,000; Harvard College, $10,000; and the Boston Museum of Fine Arts, $10,000. The housekeeper, Mary Donnellan, was given $10,000, and another house staff member also received $10,000. After some additional smaller gifts to other household staff members, the remainder of Holmes's estate, about $290,000, was given to the United States of America. Holmes considered paying taxes part of the "price of civilization," and this gift reflected that view. Unfortunately, the money was placed in the general fund of the Treasury Department, where it remained, without earning interest, for 20 years. Eventually, as a result of pressure exerted by Felix Frankfurter, who had himself become a Supreme Court justice in 1939, Holmes's gift was used to commission a series of books on the history of the Supreme Court of the United States, known as the *Oliver Wendell Holmes Devise History.* Once again Frankfurter had played a role in keeping Holmes's name before the public.

EPILOGUE

In December 1927, when Holmes was 86 years old, in his 25th year as a justice of the Supreme Court, and in his 45th year as a judge, he received a letter from Felix Frankfurter, who was 46 at the time and a member of the faculty at Harvard Law School. Frankfurter had, ever since 1912, made it a habit of writing to Holmes on his birthday and other celebratory moments. His letter read as follows:

> On Thursday the Court and you are celebrat-
> ing your silver wedding anniversary—the date of
> taking your seat being the effective date. And what
> a quarter of a century it has been. Its achievement
> will remain golden as long as the history of your
> court and of our country will endure.
> And now for the beginning of the second
> quarter century.

The letter was characteristic of the tone Frankfurter adopted in letters to Holmes, a tone that had been estab-lished when Frankfurter had first sought out Holmes's company as a 31-year-old lawyer in Washington in 1912. It was a tone of effusive flattery, of grandiose claims for

Justices of the Supreme Court viewing a model of the new Supreme Court building during the 1930 term, with Justice Brandeis on the far left, Chief Justice Hughes third from the left, and Holmes fourth from the left. The Supreme Court first held arguments in its new building in 1936, a year after Holmes's death.

Holmes's reputation, and of regular reminders that Frankfurter was Holmes's devoted acolyte and friend.

Holmes had repeatedly declared himself to be a philosophical skeptic, one who was unsure about the meaning of truth, which he once defined as "the sum of my intellectual limitations." One might have expected him to view Frankfurter's praise of him with comparable skepticism. Holmes wrote back:

> You lead me to repeat what perhaps I have repeated before—from what I said to the president when he gave me the Roosevelt medal. "For five minutes you make me believe that the dream of a lifetime has come true." But so long as one writes decisions he is concerned with the future and never can be sure that he won't find out that he really is a damn fool after all. Meantime I appreciate and love your generous attitude and know that it does you honor while reserving judgement as to No. 1....

There was some skepticism expressed in the letter: Holmes spoke of Frankfurter's praise, and of the high honor of the Presidential Medal of Freedom (he had been the first judge ever to receive the award) as making him feel that "the dream of a lifetime has come true," but only "for five minutes." Immediately his thoughts turned to his work as a judge, and the fact that judicial decisions, although intended as authoritative statements of law that are supposed to endure and to give guidance for future generations, often become obsolete or are overruled because they express a point of view that has grown out of favor.

But the most important phrase in Holmes's letter read "never can be sure that he won't find out that he really is a damn fool after all." The most impressive thing about Holmes's life, one could argue, was that when he died, two days before his 94th birthday, he was very far from finding out that he was a fool. In other words, he was very far from finding out that the ideas that he had begun to express as a young lawyer and scholar in the 1870s, that he had brought with him to the Supreme Judicial Court of Massachusetts, that he had revised and refined as a Supreme Court justice, and that he had rendered in numerous arresting versions in his letters and his public addresses were becoming obsolete. On the contrary, Holmes's intellectual and professional life had witnessed the evolving, growing acceptance of his ideas about law, judging, and free speech by a wider and wider segment of the public. He had started out as an ambitious young scholar, determined to write an original, different sort of treatment of U.S. law. When *The Common Law* was published, very few people read it, but little by little its audience grew, and the freshness of some of its passages remains to audiences at the end of the 20th century.

Holmes began his judicial career thinking that life as a judge would be the equivalent of life as a soldier, dealing with the elemental forces of the world. He soon found it had its tedious and obscure features. Nonetheless, he persevered, churning out his opinions and inserting his memorable epigrams, and somehow he came to the attention of one President, in office only by chance, who happened to nominate him to the Supreme Court. Again he plunged into the obscure business of writing opinions, but in the process he developed an attitude that ultimately called for deference toward legislation regulating economic affairs and an aggressive scrutiny of legislation regulating speech—an attitude that was not altogether logically consistent but became resonant with many 20th-century Americans.

When Holmes was nominated to the Supreme Court, his tendency to infuse his legal opinions with pithy, sometimes obscure, literary flourishes was criticized by commentators. By the time he retired he had found a large popular audience for his literary expressions. In fact, for most Americans those expressions singled him out from his fellow justices. He had become a poet on the bench, just as his father had been a poet who also practiced medicine.

In the years since Holmes's death a number of ideas about law, judging, and what makes a judge a celebrated popular figure have changed. Not many of Holmes's leading opinions are still treated as important legal precedents. Holmes himself, born in 1841, still wearing high collars and swallowtail coats in his 90s, seems anything but a modern judge, even though one of his law clerks, Alger Hiss, died only in 1996. In some respects it seems easier to believe that Holmes knew John Quincy Adams, the sixth President of the United States, than that he worked with a man who lived into the 1990s.

But Holmes's ideas have endured. The most remarkable thing about Holmes is not his longevity, nor the span of his acquaintances, nor the consistent good fortune that he had in both his career and the rest of his life, nor even his marvelous way with words. It is the remarkable way in which the ideas that he developed early in his life matured and expanded in their influence as his life evolved. In his late 20s Holmes was fighting for recognition; at 40 he finally completed his only book; at 61 he was nominated to the Supreme Court of the United States; at 90 his ideas were at the height of their acceptance and he was truly a public celebrity. Few people who live as long as Holmes avoid the unpleasant realization that the ideas they developed and cherished over the course of their lifetime have come to be regarded as obsolete. As he grew older Holmes liked to mention, in his letters, the possibility of his death, and periodically worried about being thought a "damn fool." But death came quietly for him, and his obsolescence has not yet come and may never arrive.

CHRONOLOGY

March 8, 1841

Oliver Wendell Holmes Jr. is born in Boston, Massachusetts

1857

Enters Harvard College with the class of 1861

1861

Graduates from Harvard; enlists in the 20th Regiment of Massachusetts Volunteers and receives his first Civil War wound

1862

Returns to active service in March; is wounded again in September

1863

Returns again to active service; receives his third wound in May

1864

Resigns from military service in July; enters Harvard Law School in September

1866

Receives an LL.B. degree from Harvard in June; becomes affiliated with the Boston law firm of George Shattuck

March 4, 1867

Is formally admitted to the practice of law in Massachusetts

June 17, 1872

Marries Fanny Bowditch Dixwell

March 3, 1881

The Common Law is published five days before Holmes's 40th birthday

November 1881

Accepts a professorship at Harvard Law School

1882

Begins teaching at Harvard Law School in September; resigns in December to accept the position of associate justice on the Supreme Judicial Court of Massachusetts

1887–89

Holmes's mother and sister die; he and his wife move into his father's house

July 1899

Becomes Chief Judge of the Supreme Judicial Court of Massachusetts

1894

Holmes Sr. dies.

1902

Is nominated to the Supreme Court of the United States by Theodore Roosevelt in July; is formally confirmed in December

1905

Writes dissent in *Lochner* v. *New York*

1912

Contemplates retiring from Supreme Court; Felix Frankfurter makes his acquaintance in Washington

1919

Writes opinions in the free-speech cases *Schenck* v. *United States* and *Abrams* v. *United States*

1920

Collected Legal Papers, a collection of speeches and essays, is published

1924

Receives the Roosevelt (now Presidential) Medal of Freedom, the first U.S. judge to be so honored

April 30, 1929

Fanny Holmes dies at the age of 89

March 8, 1931

Celebrates his 90th birthday with a nationwide radio address

January 12, 1932

Resigns from the Supreme Court

March 6, 1935

Dies of bronchial pneumonia at his home in Washington, D.C.

FURTHER READING

BY OLIVER WENDELL HOLMES JR.

Holmes, Oliver Wendell. *Collected Legal Papers.* Reprint, Magnolia, Mass.: Peter Smith, 1990.

Howe, Mark DeWolfe, ed. *The Common Law.* Reprint, Mineola, N.Y.: Dover Publications, 1962.

————, ed. *Holmes-Laski Letters, 1916–1935.* 2 vols. New York: Simon & Schuster, 1943.

————, ed. *Holmes-Pollock Letters, 1874–1932.* Littleton, Colo.: Fred B. Rothman, 1961.

————, ed. *The Occasional Speeches of Justice Oliver Wendell Holmes.* Cambridge: Harvard University Press, 1962.

————. *Touched with Fire: Civil War Letters and Diary of Oliver Wendell Holmes, Jr., 1861–1864.* New York: Da Capo Press, 1943.

Kellogg, Frederic Rogers, ed. *The Formative Essays of Justice Holmes.* Westport, Conn.: Greenwood, 1984.

Lerner, Max. *The Mind and Faith of Justice Holmes,* 2d ed. Piscataway, N.J.: Transaction Publishers, 1988.

Lief, Alfred. *Representative Opinions of Mr. Justice Holmes.* New York: Vanguard Press, 1931.

Mennel, Robert M., and Christine L. Compston, eds. *Holmes and Frankfurter, Their Correspondence, 1912–1934.* Hanover, N.H.: University Press of New England, 1996.

Posner, Richard A., ed. *The Essential Holmes.* Chicago: University of Chicago Press, 1992.

Shriver, Harry C., ed. *The Judicial Opinions of Oliver Wendell Holmes … as Given in the Supreme Judicial Court of Massachusetts.* Buffalo, N.Y.: William S. Hein, 1940.

ABOUT HOLMES'S LIFE AND CAREER

Baker, Liva. *The Justice from Beacon Hill.* New York: HarperCollins, 1991.

Gordon, Robert, ed. *The Legacy of Oliver Wendell Holmes, Jr.* Stanford: Stanford University Press, 1992.

Hoffheimer, Michael. *Justice Holmes and the Natural Law.* New York: Garland, 1993.

Howe, Mark DeWolfe. *Justice Oliver Wendell Holmes: The Proving Years.* Cambridge, Mass.: Harvard University Press, 1963.
———. *Justice Oliver Wendell Holmes: The Shaping Years.* Cambridge, Mass.: Harvard University Press, 1957.
Monagan, John. *The Grand Panjandrum: The Mellow Years of Justice Holmes.* Lanham, Md.: University Press of America, 1988.
White, G. Edward. *Justice Oliver Wendell Holmes: Law and the Inner Self.* New York: Oxford University Press, 1993.

ABOUT THE SUPREME COURT

Hall, Kermit L. *The Oxford Companion to the Supreme Court of the United States.* New York: Oxford University Press, 1992.
Patrick, John J. *The Young Oxford Companion to the Supreme Court of the United States.* New York: Oxford University Press, 1994.
Urofsky, Melvin I. *A March of Liberty: A Constitutional History of the United States.* New York: McGraw-Hill, 1994.
White, G. Edward. *The American Judicial Tradition: Profiles of Leading American Judges.* 2d. ed. New York: Oxford University Press, 1988.
Wiecek, William. *Liberty in Law: The Supreme Court in American Life.* Baltimore: Johns Hopkins University Press, 1988.

INDEX

ACKNOWLEDGMENTS

This book has been a different writing experience for me and has given me an enhanced appreciation for the authors of books intended for a young adult audience. One likes to think that years in academic life have not deprived one of the ability to write with some clarity and zest, but there is sometimes a tendency to pick up bad habits. Thanks to Tara Deal for her vigilance in the service of accessible prose.

Oliver Wendell Holmes: Sage of the Supreme Court is the brainchild of my longtime friend Nancy Toff at Oxford University Press, and Nancy was also helpful in smoothing transitions from one sort of Oxford book to another. Thanks also to Casper Grathwohl and Karen S. Fein at Oxford for coordinating details of the editorial and production processes.

Professor Laurin A. Wollan, Jr. of the School of Criminology and Criminal Justice at Florida State University was kind enough to assign a manuscript draft of the book to several of his students for their reactions, and I profited from their comments. My special thanks to Larry for volunteering his services.

As always, my family has found numerous ways to keep me from becoming too engrossed with writing projects. My love to Susan Davis White, Alexandra Valre White, Elisabeth McCafferty Davis White, and John and Jane Davis. This book might actually be one a majority of family members will read. I regret that Frances McCafferty White, a former high school English teacher who would certainly have read it, did not live to see its completion. She would have enjoyed the prospect of one of her son's books showing up in a school library. Let's hope it gets checked out now and then.

G.E.W.
Charlottesville
May 1999

PICTURE CREDITS

TEXT CREDITS

An Autobiographical Sketch, p. 22: Oliver Wendell Holmes, Jr., *Harvard College, Class of 1861 Album,* 329 Harvard University Archives.

"I Thought I Was Dying," pp. 28–29: Oliver Wendell Holmes, Jr., diary entry [date unknown], in Mark DeWolfe Howe, ed., *Touched with Fire: Civil War Letters and Diary of Oliver Wendell Holmes, Jr., 1861–1864,* p. 23 (1946).

"The Life of the Law Has Not Been Logic," p. 55: Oliver Wendell Holmes, Jr., *The Common Law* 1 (1881).

An Unexpected Dissent, p. 93: *Northern Securities Company* v. *United States,* 193 U.S. 197 (1904) (Justice Holmes, dissenting).

"They Do Not Create Something Out of Nothing," p. 99: *Plant* v. *Woods,* 176 Mass. 492 (1900) (Chief Justice Holmes, dissenting).

The Case for Majority Rule, p. 102: *Lochner* v. *New York,* 198 U.S. 45 (1905) (Justice Holmes, dissenting).

Shocking Speech, p. 125: James B. Peabody, ed., *Holmes-Einstein Letters*, pp. 243–45 (1964).

"I Have Had My Reward," p. 131: James B. Peabody, ed., *Holmes-Einstein Letters,* pp. 297–98 (1964).

G. Edward White is University Professor and John B. Minor Professor of Law and History at the University of Virginia. Four of his books have won Gavel Awards from the American Bar Association. His *The Marshall Court and Cultural Change* won the James Willard Hurst Prize of the Law and Society Association and *Justice Holmes: Law and the Inner Self* won the Littleton-Griswold Award of the American Historical Association and the Scribes Award of the American Society of Writers on Legal Subjects. In 1996 White received the Triennial Coif Award of the American Association of American Law Schools for distinguished scholarship.